16.
Vidya

Vidya has a master's degree in linguistics and is keenly interested in contemporary theatre and cinema. She currently works for a voluntary organization engaged in serving destitute people in Chennai.

LIVING SMILE VIDYA

I am Vidya

A Transgender's Journey

RUPA

Published by
Rupa Publications India Pvt. Ltd 2013
7/16, Ansari Road, Daryaganj
New Delhi 110002

Sales Centres:

Allahabad Bengaluru Chennai
Hyderabad Jaipur Kathmandu
Kolkata Mumbai

Copyright © New Horizon Media Pvt. Ltd 2007, 2013

First published by New Horizon Media Pvt. Ltd 2007. This edition
published by arrangement with the original publisher.

All rights reserved.
No part of this publication may be reproduced, transmitted,
or stored in a retrieval system, in any form or by any means,
electronic, mechanical, photocopying, recording or otherwise,
without the prior permission of the publisher.

ISBN: 978-81-291-2398-5

10 9 8 7 6 5 4 3 2 1

Printed at Parksons Graphics Pvt. Ltd, Mumbai

This book is sold subject to the condition that it shall not,
by way of trade or otherwise, be lent, resold, hired out, or otherwise
circulated, without the publisher's prior consent, in any form of binding or
cover other than that in which it is published.

Contents

Nirvana

I love the window seat in trains. Stretching my legs, I was enjoying the landscape—the trees and plants, the buildings—as it flashed past me. It was a pleasure akin to the first cup of lazy coffee on a holiday.

'Where are you headed?' The unexpected question woke me from my reverie. I looked up.

It was a rozwala—a regular commuter. One look at my ordinary clothes, and he must have decided that I did not belong in the sleeper compartment, that I was, perhaps, a ticketless traveller.

One wore the most basic clothes on one's way to the operation we call nirvana. The same applied to jewellery. That's why I had on the oldest sari I had: a white one printed with blue flowers. My tiny nose stud was all the gold I was wearing. I would have to hand it over to Sugandhi Ayah after the operation tomorrow.

'Baithoon idhar?' The rozwala was asking if he could sit beside me.

I was pretty sure he thought I didn't have a ticket. Still, his manner had been polite, so I made room for him by shifting my legs and went back to looking out of the window.

My train ticket from Pune to Cuddapah had been booked at

Lonavala station the very day after Nani agreed to send me for my nirvana. That day, I didn't perform my dhandha—begging. The whole thing was surprisingly different from the norm—usually no Nani planned a nirvana down to the last detail a month in advance. And no tirunangai—transgender—made advance train reservations for the operation.

'You have to be discreet in such matters—observe great secrecy,' Sugandhi Ayah was in a plaintive mood, complaining non-stop. 'Girls nowadays don't listen to their elders; they do exactly as they please.' She was constantly comparing and contrasting transgenders of the past and present, adding to the pathos by relating some personal experiences from her own life.

Sugandhi had a massive physique. She wore her salt and pepper hair in a tight bun and the two-rupee-coin sized kumkum bindi on her broad forehead instilled awe in onlookers; her mouth constantly chewed paan, while her bell-like voice matched her impressive physical appearance—Sugandhi Ayah looked formidable. Satya and I sometimes took the liberty of teasing her, calling her grandma, and she allowed us indulgently. Today she was taking us and Nagarani, our next door neighbour, to our nirvana.

Sarada Nani was an important person in the Pune locality where a large population of transgenders lived. I was a chela daughter of one of her chela daughters, Aruna Amma. Satya was older, my senior in the transgender group. She was of a swarthy complexion, solidly built—like Sugandhi Ayah—with a voice to match and long, thick hair. She was an excellent cook. Despite her seniority, her operation was going to take place only now. That my nirvana was scheduled along with hers was a big step for me—my hair was still too short to tie up in a bun at that time.

Satya did not show as much interest as I did in the nirvana. It wasn't clear who would accompany her, so I reserved only my train berth. All that was not so important, though—any old ticket would do for Sugandhi Ayah and Satya. They sat on a newspaper they spread near the compartment door and answered the TTE's queries. Nagarani huddled close to them and they managed to stay there till morning.

I got up after a while and joined them. The old woman continued to tell oft-repeated tales of woe from her life, of her trials and tribulations. They assumed new dimensions that evening for all three of us. As she went on with accounts of nirvana and its after-effects, we listened in terror.

I went to my berth when Ayah was overcome by sleep. Just one more night: tomorrow would dawn the fruition of my desires, the fulfilment of my dreams. The night was long. I tossed and turned. I woke up and looked around—the whole train was asleep. Very few people were awake—the engine driver, a few policemen on patrol duty, and I.

Nirvana! How long I had waited for it! What humiliation I had suffered! Obsessed with it, I had mortgaged my pride, my anger, my honour—I had even begged on the streets to achieve that end. How could I sleep now, with my dream about to be fulfilled tomorrow?

Morning at last: I welcomed the new day eagerly, with not a trace of fatigue, even though I had kept awake all night. I drank a cup of coffee—Sugandhi Ayah had warned me to take only fluids in preparation for the operation.

It was the most important day of my life. Autorickshaws mobbed us as the four of us emerged from the railway station. It was the 26th of April.

'Naganna or Bapanna?' Hordes of drivers pounced on us with their incessant questioning. We managed to stave off the competing marauders and, negotiating the fare with one of them, got into an autorickshaw.

'Ayah, how do they know we are going to one of those doctors?' I asked Sugandhi.

'Even the newborns here know our kind come to Cuddapah for the operation,' Nagarani said.

'Right down to the doctor's name? Tell me, Ayah, which doctor are we going to?'

There was no reply from Sugandhi Ayah.

'Why are you so glum, Ayah?'

'Shut up.'

I had no choice. I kept watching the Telugu film posters. As we got off the autorickshaw, I was filled with happiness at our arrival to the Cuddapah nursing home.

'Hurry up.' All of a sudden, Ayah rushed us in. The nursing home was right on the street. Though not a main road, it was busy. The cinema across the road displayed a poster for *Chandramukhi*.

The hospital was abuzz with activity. We were herded upstairs through what was evidently a rear stairwell. A nursing home attendant accompanied us, talking all the while in Telugu to Sugandhi Ayah. *She must be a frequent visitor here*, I said to myself. The attendant left us in a room.

There were three steel cots in that room, which had an adjacent bathroom equipped with a solitary bucket. The cots were bare, with no mattresses or sheets on them.

Many female names were scrawled on the wall—some in ink, others in charcoal. The room seemed to be reserved exclusively for transgenders. Our predecessors had scribbled their names on the wall, presumably because they feared they would die on the operation table. That was their way of ensuring the survival of at least their names after the hazardous operation we called nirvana.

'Write your name on the wall, if you like,' Sugandhi Ayah said.

I didn't feel like doing so—I was certain I would live. Hadn't I struggled all the while just for this? I was hungry.

Sugandhi was the only one who had had eaten since last night. The three of us had obeyed her instructions to fast.

'Go to the bathroom now if you must. Once in the operation theatre, your stomach should be completely empty,' Sugandhi Ayah warned us. Nagarani looked scared. I watched Satya. She looked grim as usual. I was all aflutter—*When? When?* The tension was palpable. None of us minded the strange odour in the room. Apprehension gripped us.

We waited for a while. A male attendant came to Sugandhi. He said something to her and went away. We were watching all the while. Ayah then took all three of us downstairs. They took blood from each of us for a blood test.

'We'll get the blood test report in half an hour,' Sugandhi Ayah said. 'They will do the operation once the report shows you are HIV negative. The operation won't take more than half an hour.'

Would there be no more tests? Wouldn't they test us for BP, blood sugar? Only AIDS? Nagarani asked, 'Why, won't they operate if we have AIDS?'

'Do you see Janaki in the next room? She has AIDS, they say. They collected an extra two thousand rupees from her to do the operation.' Only after Sugandhi Ayah pointed her out did I see the woman lying there post-operation.

I went in and saw her. She was from my street. Though she had been in Pune for many years, she still retained the flavour of the village. Her language had remained unchanged: she had lived in Mumbai and Pune for five years or so, but couldn't speak a whole sentence in Hindi. I didn't know her very well, but I had seen her being heckled while walking on the street. It was a rude shock to Satya and me to know she had AIDS.

The three of us chattered nervously for a while, anticipating the moment anxiously.

'Who's going first?' Sugandhi Ayah asked. I couldn't bear it any longer.

'I'll go first, Ayah!' I shouted, 'Let me go.'

Ayah came to a decision. 'Satya is your senior, let her go first, you go after her,' she said. No one replied. It was frustrating to know we had to wait longer.

'Akka, let me go first, Akka, please.'

'Ok, go. I don't mind. Ask the hag.'

Sugandhi Ayah was particular about seniority. There was no point in pleading with her.

The blood test results were out by then. Ayah handed over the report to each of us, asking us to keep it carefully. Thank God, none of us had AIDS.

Speaking in Telugu, a hospital attendant called Satya and asked Nagarani and me to wait. He told us to change and be ready—to strip down to our skirts.

Ayah had already coached us. They took Satya away.

'When will the operation be over? How long will it take?' I kept asking Ayah.

I wasn't prepared for the speed of the operation. I expected an operation to take at least an hour, and a vital one like ours at least two hours. In barely twenty minutes, a man and a woman wheeled Satya out—it was all over. Neither attendant looked like a nurse or a hospital worker. You'd think they belonged to some completely unrelated profession.

They lifted Satya from the wheelchair and, spreading a couple of newspapers on a steel cot, dropped her unceremoniously on it. Their unsafe, unhygienic approach made me nervous, but there was no time to worry. They whisked me away as soon as they had dumped Satya on the cot.

'Keep repeating the name of the Mother during the operation,' Ayah told me as I left for the operation theatre.

But it was no operation theatre, I realized as soon as I entered the tiny room—it was a slaughterhouse. 'Mata, mata, mata,' I repeated to myself. In the room was a solitary cot. A masked doctor stood by its side; his eyes were those of an old man. Two more people—a man and a woman—filled the minuscule room. There was no way another person could enter the room.

I wanted to talk to the doctor, but the environment silenced me. They removed my skirt, made me lie down on the cot, and helped me overcome my embarrassment. They made me curl into the embryonic posture, and gave me a spinal injection. It hurt. I lay down straight and was given a glucose drip through a vein in my right arm.

I was able to cooperate with the staff, as Senbagam—who had undergone the surgery a few months ago—had given me a detailed account of the various steps. She had warned me that the spinal shot would anaesthetize me below the waist, so I was quite brave.

Only when the surgeon made the first incision on my abdomen with his scalpel did I realize I hadn't quite lost sensation altogether. Another spinal injection followed my screams of pain. The pain subsided but did not disappear. I couldn't move my hands and legs, but I felt the movements of the surgeon's knife and my pain quite clearly.

I cursed and swore: 'I can't bear the pain, let me go!' I screamed at them constantly. I wanted to run away—I wanted to kill the doctor and his helper. Desperate with pain, I repeatedly called out to Mata as Ayah had advised me, reaching a crescendo of, 'MAAAA....TAAAA.' As the operation reached its climax, the pain rose to unbearable heights—as if someone was digging deep into my innards with a long rod and removing my intestines.

Yes, what I saw in that instant was death. They had removed that part of me over which I had shed silent tears of rejection from as far back as I could remember—my penis and my testicles had been excised.

I was sutured and daubed with medication later, all of which I could feel very distinctly.

Ah! Nirvana! The ultimate peace!

My operation took all of twenty minutes. They put me on a stretcher, writhing in pain, and carried me down a ramp accompanied by violent jerks, causing new pains and aches. They dumped me on a newspaper-covered steel cot just as they had dropped Satya before.

In the bed next to mine, I could hear her crying and moaning. Even though I was in great pain, I was able to withstand it. Soon, to my surprise, Satya began to sob uncontrollably.

Was it really Satya crying, unable to bear her pain? She had been an elder sister to me in Pune at the place where we had sought refuge. She was a strong person. Thrashed by Nani after an occasional drunken bout, she would lie down absolutely still and quiet. I couldn't believe that she was crying in pain now—or that I was able to stand the pain better.

Inside, I was at peace. It was a huge relief. I was now a woman: mine was a woman's body. Its shape would be what my heart wanted, had yearned for. This pain would obliterate all earlier pains.

I wanted to thank everyone, cry out loud to the doctor, his assistants, Sugandhi Ayah; express my gratitude to them to my heart's content. I couldn't move my lips or open my mouth.

I thanked them silently: 'Thank you for removing my maleness from my body; thank you for making my body a female body. My life is fulfilled. If I die now, I'll lose nothing. I can sleep in peace.'

The intensity of the pain grew with the hours. My abdomen seemed to be on fire. I couldn't move my arms and legs. The pain was unbearable, however hard I tried to ease it.

Amma, Amma, I have become a woman. I am not Saravanan any more, I am Vidya—a complete Vidya—a whole woman. Where are you, Amma? Can't you come to me by some miracle, at least for a moment? Please hold my hand, Amma. My heart seems to be breaking into smithereens. Radha, please Radha, I am no longer your brother, Radha. I am your sister now, your sister. Come to me, Radha. Chithi, Manju, Prabha, Appa…

Look at me Appa—look at my dissected body. This is a mere body. Can you see that I can bear all this pain? I can take any amount of pain, Appa. Look at me, Appa. Look at me as a woman. Accept me as a girl, Appa.

Only I could hear my screams.

Appa

When I was born the first time, my parents named me Saravanan. I was their sixth child, born after years of prayers for a boy. In fact, their first had been a boy, unfortunately still-born. Four girls followed, two of them succumbing to unknown diseases. Given the circumstances, I realized pretty early in life what joy my arrival must have brought my parents.

My family wasn't exactly well off. My father, Ramaswami, was known as Nattamai—or chieftain—in Puttur, next to Tiruchi. The title must have been somebody's idea of a joke, for my father was hardly any kind of a chief—certainly not the kind immortalized by Tamil cinema. He was a municipal worker of the lowest rung: a sweeper. My mother, Veeramma and he were married in 1973. They started life together in a small hut they built on an unoccupied piece of land on Attumanthai (flock of sheep) Street.

My mother was someone special. Her name meant 'brave woman', and she was every bit that. Brave and hard working, sweet tempered, she was also a typical Indian wife, who submitted to her husband's tyrannical ways. She died in an accident when I was eleven.

The pain and awareness of their oppression on the basis of their caste haunted my parents all their lives. Their intense yearning for a son must have sprung from their desperate hope that he would change the course of their abject existence.

Appa, my father, began in the business of milk supply. I remember that he had job opportunities in the police and southern railway as well, but he was not too keen on such careers; he perhaps believed he must run his own business, however small. Making ends meet was never easy. His relatives were determined he should find employment, and they repeatedly counselled him, persuading him to join the Tiruchi Refugee Camp as a sweeper.

My father's life was one of frustration—frustration that his lack of formal education beyond Class 8 had landed him in a lowly sweeper's job. For all that it was a government job. He constantly dreamed of his son growing up to be a district collector—surely the top job in India! His dreams, desires and ambitions all centred on his son of the future.

When these dreams were shattered, and his first child to survive turned out to be a daughter, Appa accepted her cheerfully.

My father adored M.G. Ramachandran, the famous film star popularly known as MGR. Who wasn't an MGR fan those days? Appa named his first daughter Radha after the leading lady in an MGR movie. Manju, his second daughter, was also named after a co-star of MGR.

My father was hoping the next baby would be a boy, to make up for two girls and the loss of his firstborn son, but that was not to be. The next two children were girls as well: Vembu and Vellachi, both of whom succumbed to mysterious ailments. This was a turning point in Appa's life, which plummeted him into the depths of despair.

For many years he had practiced his own vague brand of atheism, but he suddenly made an about-face and visited temple after temple. Landing finally at the Vayalur Murugan temple in Tiruchi, he vowed to name his next child after Murugan (the presiding deity) if it was a boy. He would also shave his head in a pious offering of his locks to the lord.

I was born on 25 March 1982. My parents named me Saravanan in fulfilment of my father's contract with Murugan—Saravanan is one of Murugan's many names.

It had been nearly ten years since my parents' wedding when I arrived, and what challenges they had to encounter during that period! Their surroundings, for one, had undergone considerable change.

Vacant land belonging to the government is known as poramboke land. Squatters often occupy such land and eventually maintain it permanently. The poramboke land on Attumanthai Street, where Appa and others had built their huts, was now a full-fledged neighbourhood: Bhupesh Gupta Nagar, in memory of a revolutionary by that name. My father, the nattamai, was responsible for the name change.

The street had grown. So had our town. The whole city had been transformed in that decade. Still, we were poor as ever. My father continued to be a municipal conservation worker, sweeping. He was eternally running from pillar to post to apply for an electricity connection for our street. At home, my mother and my sisters took care of me—spoiled me. By the time I was ready to go to school, my father had made preparations on a war footing.

I was a privileged member of the household. Of the three children, I was the one person who didn't have to do any work at home. That was the unwritten law. I enjoyed every kind of concession.

'The only work we want you to do is study,' Appa said.

'Remember, it's your job to study.' He was quite the dictator when it came to my education, allowing no discussion.

'If any of you dares to give him work that interferes with

his studies, I'll kill you,' he warned us.

My two sisters—ten-year-old Radha and six-year-old Manju—were so terrified of Appa's threat that they never let me do any household work. I was the male heir of the family, and that was reason enough to exempt me from work of any kind! My doting mother carried me around until I was five years old. When he came back from work in the evening, Appa usually brought us sweets and snacks, and you could bet he slipped in something extra for me every time.

I don't remember my sisters ever being jealous of me. In fact, they showered me with love. From the time she was born, Radha had grown up amidst my parents' constant prayers for a male child. From a tender age, I remember her as a second mother to me. When Amma died, Radha took over altogether.

Radha was a goddess to all of us. She took charge of the house as soon as my parents went to work everyday. Able to cook when barely ten, she swept and swabbed the house, washed the dishes and our clothes, stored water—took care of everything, basically. We should in all fairness have treasured her, treated her like royalty, though we did not. Instead, I was the sole beneficiary of all the love and affection at home by virtue of being a boy.

Amazingly, not once did I hear either Radha or Manju criticize this overt partiality. I think they came to believe in time that looking after me was the very purpose of their existence.

For my part, I studied well, to Appa's great joy. My academic excellence in contrast with my sisters' unschooled ways gave him immense pride. I was ranked first in my class in the first grade. When Appa came home and heard the news, he carried me on his shoulders and went round and round Bhupesh Gupta Nagar, broadcasting the news to the world: 'My son got the first rank,' he announced again and again.

I remember the day so clearly. Appa loved me but he had

never carried me or fondled me before. His public demonstration of love for me that day was the best reward I could have asked for. My stock in the neighbourhood shot up—I was the boy who was ranked first in his class.

My academic feats complicated life for my sisters. When Amma left for work at five o'clock in the morning, it was Radha's duty to wake me up to make me study. She had no escape from that responsibility, for if I did not study, Radha or Manju would be spanked even harder than I would be.

Up that early, I studied for an hour. Manju went out at six o'clock to buy tea and porai biscuits. Radha swept the house and started cooking by then, while Manju cleaned the vessels. I had to continue studying till 7.30, when Appa woke up. The girls then had to ensure I bathed, ate my breakfast, got ready and dashed off to school.

Appa gave Radha our daily allowance of one rupee every morning. My share was forty paise while my sisters each got thirty. They could not go to their classrooms without depositing me at mine. As soon as I came home, I had to do my homework, after which commenced Appa's lessons for me.

Appa made me do third grade exercises when I was still in the first grade. He made me do the multiplication tables—from one to twenty—ten times every day. 'Do you know Abraham Lincoln studied under the street light and became president of America?' he repeated constantly. He made me believe that studying hard in the light of a hurricane lamp would one day make me the district collector.

I had a natural aptitude for studies, and I was an eager student. I was doing quite well at school, but as time progressed, I began to resent Appa's constant harassment—both mental and physical. I knew he was only doing what was good for me, but losing the simple joys and freedom other children enjoyed irritated me. Was a childhood without games worth living? Home was a virtual prison—even the love of my mother and sisters could not bend its bars.

My father never allowed me to play with boys and girls. I could not understand this blanket ban, and wondered if it was because the kids in our neighbourhood were poor students. Unlike our neighbours, my father gave education a great deal of importance; he feared the influence of the other families in our colony upon my studies.

It was my sisters' responsibility to prevent me from giving Appa the slip and going out to play. Radha and Manju kept constant vigil over my movements, frightened of what Appa might do if I did get away. Sometimes they scolded me and even slapped me playfully if I tried to step out of line. They were so fond of me, though, that they never let me down by tattling.

When I came home from a school exam, Appa conducted the same test at home all over again. I was not even allowed to go out to play during vacations. Preparations for the next examination started immediately after the previous test had finished.

All of this work was in addition to the demands of my school teachers, who made me answer all papers at home without omitting a single question, even in multiple choice assignments. I had to do five question papers in a single day, and invariably, just when I breathed a sigh of relief at completing them, Appa's home lessons started. If I slowed down my homework to avoid Appa's exercises, he thrashed me. My body would be bruised black and blue with belt marks all over. If Amma or my sisters tried to stop him, they were belted, too. 'Weren't you expected to ensure he did his homework?' he would scream at them. I regularly wet my shorts in fear and shock.

When I was eleven, my mother died in a road accident. My grief was immeasurable, indescribable. I had been my mother's little boy, always at home, always protected by her. It was hard to come to terms with her absence all of a sudden.

Appa made matters worse by remarrying. Lata, or Thangammal, who was younger than Radha, was our new stepmother.

I was too young then to know if what Appa had done was right or wrong. Luckily, Chithi was a good person and treated me with love. My sisters, too, were a great consolation, and with their help the wounds of losing Amma healed slowly. Things gradually changed for the better—except for Appa's watching over me. As I continued to do well in school, his dreams for me grew; and as his dreams for me grew, his oppressive ways increased in intensity as well. God knows what fears and anxieties troubled him, but he never allowed me a normal childhood.

I remember this incident: I came second in my class in the sixth grade exams. I was scared beyond description that evening and could hardly sleep that night, afraid of the consequences of showing my report card to my father the next morning. When I finally drifted into a fitful sleep, I dreamt of Appa belting me. Waking, I found I had wet the bed.

As the day dawned, I had no choice but to show Appa my report card. The paper trembled with me as I handed it over to him. I received the cruellest punishment of my life that morning.

Remember how Appa carried me around Bhupesh Gupta Nagar the day I was ranked first in the class? Today, unable to bear what he saw as the first crumbling of his dreams, he lifted me much the same way again. Only this time he dropped me forcefully from a height. He then kicked me in my stomach—I was terror stricken.

He picked me up and thrashed me wildly. My Chithi and sisters, who tried to protect me, were thrashed as well. Our pain and tears and screams had no effect on him.

Second rank! Something he had never imagined I would get. It made no sense to me. How could I explain to my father that not much divided the first and second ranks?

He would never understand. He did not. He smashed me around until he got his fury out of his system.

I was a complete mess; beaten black and blue, no strength left in me, I sought refuge in my sister's lap. Why didn't I have a loving father like other children? The question comes back to haunt me even today, whenever I see caring men.

The princess

I am the princess,
A fresh new rose.
Will my dream come true?

The radio was playing the popular film song and I was dancing to the tune, wearing Manju's Indian skirt. At six or seven, I didn't fully understand the meaning of the words, but I enjoyed their lilt and tenderness. I was at my grandmother's house on Attumanthai Street. My father's two younger brothers and two sisters lived there as well. I usually locked myself inside once all of them had gone out, put on girls' clothes and sang and danced. I loved it.

As thrilling as dancing was pirouetting at a rapid pace and sitting down with force so that the long skirt spread out like a lotus, on which I then seemed to be seated.

When I was spinning round and round one day with just such exhilarating abandon, my grandmother, who had gone out, came back into the house. 'Oh my God,' she blurted out.

'Look at this madness. Girls, come and see what this boy is up to.' Grandma probably thought I was doing some playful imitation. Hardly did she know the true story, did she?

In Bhupesh Gupta Nagar we had no television, because we

had no electricity. Every home had a portable transistor radio, however, and we too had a Philips. Sometimes, when I had finished my homework, and thought he was in a rare good mood, I begged Appa for permission to go and watch TV at my Chitappa's house on Attumanthai Street.

'Okay, just for half an hour,' Appa would say. 'You must come back and study. You must show the same interest in studies that you have in watching TV. Understand?' Permission was always accompanied by bullying!

Instantly, Radha, Manju and I ran to Chitappa's house. That was the pre-cable TV era. The treat that awaited us was the famous song and dance sequence programme, or sometimes the Sunday movie on Doordarshan.

Chitappa's house was not a thatched hut like ours: it was a tiled house, which has now grown into a two-storey building. It had electricity; it had fans; it had a TV. We often went there with Appa's half-hearted permission, or occasionally by giving him the slip, to sit in front of the idiot box in a trance, to watch *Oliyum Oliyum* or *Light and Sound*—the film song sequence programme we were ready to die for.

I loved cinema. I loved the charisma of the heroes, their style, their majesty and their valour. However, what attracted me most and caused me painful yearning was the beauty of the leading ladies: I adored their sweet Tamil, and their gait. When watching, I floated in an imaginary world in which I blushed as they did, danced and wooed their heroes as they did, expressed anger as they did. Once I emerged from the dream and re-entered the real world, I masqueraded as the heroines, dressing and walking around like them.

In this, I was aided and abetted by my sister Manju's skirts and midis, her eyeshadow, bangles, bindis and costume jewels. Lipstick was easily replicated by applying coconut oil to my lips and rubbing it in repeatedly. Long, plaited hair was an altogether different issue, but I knew how to overcome that problem too: just spread a thin cotton towel—a large kerchief, really (the kind that is common among ordinary folk, and not like Turkish towels)—on your head like a veil, not covering the forehead, and twirl the long rear portion as if it were covering a pigtail. Worn this way, you could easily pass as a girl drying her hair after a shower.

Though I indulged in my antics in careful secrecy, I got caught in the act sometimes. My family did not take it too seriously in the beginning. They put it down as innocent pranks of a child and scolded me occasionally, but they saw no cause for alarm at the time.

Our hut in Bhupesh Nagar had two parts, like two dwellings. The first one had a small, doorless room—it was a kitchen-cum-bedroom with two mud-stoves and a cot. The store room had a rice barrel, a wooden almirah with vessels, water cans and a loft. The 'second' house was a single room in which we had a cupboard and a trunk containing our clothes. There was a central thatched portion, with a broad pyol or thinnai, with a bathroom next to it. The entrance to each portion faced the others to form a kind of circle, and in the middle was the main door. Between the middle and big portions was a footpath.

We children slept on the cot in the kitchen.

The three of us were reading our schoolbooks, still huddled under our blankets one cold morning, when a young man from our neighbourhood came running into our house. Obviously tense, he asked Appa and all of us to go with him. We didn't know what it was all about, but it was obviously bad news.

Soon we were at the government hospital. Amma, when leaving for work, had met with an accident, and her condition was said to be serious. When the ambulance arrived, she appeared to be peacefully asleep.

It had been such a quiet morning at home. By noon, it was filled with relatives and our neighbours. In the midst of the wails and laments of the mourners, Amma was laid out on a cot in front of the house, where Radha and Manju sat at her feet. They were both weeping. Appa must have been crying in some corner—I couldn't find him, but I knew he could not bear the loss of Amma. For all that he terrorized her, kicked her and beat her, she was the strong one in the family. She had great willpower. She might have looked like a fool to accept all the taunts and beatings, but she thought domestic problems should not be taken to the street. Her dignity was something everyone had come to recognize. People approached her with respect.

It was she who lay there. I was at an age when I did not fully comprehend the extent of our loss. I wanted to cry; I cried. People trying to comfort me seemed to cry even more. They hugged me more than they normally did and wept.

'Poor boy, poor boy.' They were overflowing with sympathy for me.

I stayed there for a while, then got up quietly. I felt no one would take any notice of me whatever I did, so I went into the middle house, put on one of Manju's skirts, shut the door and started to dance.

I am the king's daughter,
A fresh new rose.
Will my dreams come true?

I danced for a long time—I cannot remember how long. Sensing the gaze of someone looking at me, I turned to find Fathima Akka peering through the window. She was about Manju's age, and lived on our street.

'Yuck! Look at Saravanan. He's dancing wearing a girl's clothes,' she cried.

Now the story was out in the open.

'What are you doing, dancing like a girl at such an unhappy time?' Appa slapped me.

In the evening, Amma was carried out into the street in the midst of all the chaos. Our next-door neighbour, Balammakka, carried me on her waist. All the mourners stopped at the end of the street while the pall bearers went ahead, carrying Amma. The crowd blocked my view, so Balammakka lifted me high enough to watch Amma wend away. I was in a panic, trembling, asking 'where's Amma going?' and realizing she would never come back.

A home without Amma—me without Amma: impossible; a terrible betrayal.

'Amma, Amma, I want you! Please leave me alone! I want Amma!' My screams pierced the neighbourhood.

I hadn't cried since the morning.

My father's second wife, our Chithi, joined us within a year of Amma's death. The year after that, my new sister, Prabha, was born.

There was as yet no major change in my habits, but I started noticing a difference in the way people approached me—the way they looked at me. My old ways—the same habits which had been dismissed lightly as childish pranks—were now viewed with disfavour. Chithi and Radha scolded me for my acts, and Appa thrashed me regularly.

'What's wrong with my preferences? Why should a boy only wear shirts and trousers? I like skirts and blouses. Why can't I wear them? Why do people find something odd in what comes to me naturally?'

Once I asked Appa to buy me a midi and a gown. 'Please buy me the same clothes you buy for Radha and Manju,' I asked him, confident he would oblige. He normally indulged my whims so long as I did my best in my studies, so I wasn't prepared for the terrible beating that followed.

Deciding it was unsafe to wear a skirt and dance, I enjoyed other pleasures in private. One activity I liked was wrapping a towel all the way up my chest, just as film heroines did in bathing scenes—I started doing that regularly, preening myself in front of a mirror.

Gradually, both family and neighbours started noticing my unusual behaviour. My habits of wearing drag, bathing with the towel wrapped around my chest, tying a towel around my head to dry my imaginary long hair—all this was now public knowledge. My voice was still soft and effeminate, and I tended to blush, gesture and walk like a woman, too. All this only added to my problems.

People were mostly sympathetic, as I was a motherless child and a good student. Some of them teased me regularly. Rasalu Akka, who lived nearby, repeatedly made fun of me, calling me a sissy, or 'girly'—Actually I didn't mind being called 'girly'—it gave me a secret thrill. When I walked down the street, youngsters started teasing me: 'Look at the nattamai's son. He walks like a female!'

The teasing did not hurt me. On the contrary, it pleased me. It made me happy to know that at least some onlookers understood what I was feeling.

Other boys played the usual boys' games with marbles, tops and kites, but I preferred to join the girls at their games—generally board games like dayakattam (the Indian version of Chinese checkers) and pallanguzhi. I loved playing girls' games and being one of them.

I liked being with the girls from my class—Kanmani, Kavita, Amritavalli and Indumati—more than I enjoyed the company of the boys of my school—that of Chezhian, Vijay and Kumaresan. At school, I was known as a nerd, Appurani and a coward. All the girls I have mentioned here were good students. In particular, I had special respect for Amritavalli. She resembled the Tamil movie star of yesteryear, K.R. Vijaya. I liked her thick double plaits and her smile—though I cannot deny some envy of her. We once had a dance contest during lunch break, wherein we both danced on numbers we knew. The students who watched us thought mine was the better performance. Their appreciation gave me the perverse satisfaction of winning a point over Amritavalli.

On another occasion, my friends from our street and I staged a mock play, in which I performed a snake dance in imitation of Sripriya in the film *Neeya* (a box office hit of the time). I was already enamoured of a career as a film heroine.

When I was in the eighth grade, Radha got married. It was a shattering blow. She had been everything to me after Amma's death.

Chithi tried to comfort me: 'Don't cry,' she said, 'Akka still lives nearby.' She was right, of course. So why did I miss Akka so much? I had no answer.

I went to the Puttur Fathima Middle School earlier, and moved to Bishop Heber in ninth grade. Bishop Heber was a boys' school that went all the way to grade twelve.

My effeminate ways—hitherto an object of ridicule on my street—now became the target of my schoolmates' taunts. Even kids from lower classes teased me at school: 'Look at this lady,' they shouted after me. It became quite common for the boys to trouble me. I was still a bright student, but I was lonely through high school. My studies began to suffer.

Adults were no better. My effeminate speech and behaviour, the fact that I preferred the company of girls, drew out the worst in them—they, like my schoolmates, started using my femininity as an excuse to insult me. It made me wary of the external world and increased my loneliness. I retreated to a world of my own creation. My sessions of dancing to the radio in drag continued, but extremely carefully—with great secrecy.

I passed my tenth grade exams with 84% marks. For eleventh, my father put me in a different school—another branch of Bishop Heber near Rock Fort, Tiruchi. It was another boys' school.

The new school and new atmosphere were even more unfriendly than the old. I had no friends; no one to share my likes and dislikes; no one to understand me. On the contrary, there was no shortage of taunts and jibes.

Even though I was extra careful not to reveal myself, my irrepressible femininity exposed me. Once again I became an object of ridicule, and inevitably my studies were affected. For example, we stood in a definite order for the prayer assembly, and my usual place was between seventh and tenth in my class. One day I happened to be in the ninth place, and a classmate immediately pounced on the coincidence (the number nine is the offensive epithet in Tamil for eunuchs or transgenders).

'Saravana, You are Nine, isn't that why you are standing ninth?' he jeered.

Everyone laughed—I felt humiliated. After that, I was ever watchful not to stand in the ninth position at the assembly. I made sure every time that I was a different number, and only then did I breathe a sigh of relief.

Crude puns were invented by my classmates to scribble with my name on the blackboard—for instance, adding the suffix 'ali', a colloquialism for eunuchs, to regular Tamil words to describe me. Some such were padippaali and uzhaippaali. The word padippaali in Tamil means a learned person, and the word uzhaippaali an industrious person. Often when we returned after lunch to the classroom, the blackboard would carry such graffiti as 'Saravanan the padippali' or 'Saravanan the uzhaippali'—the shortening of the vowel giving the word an offensive twist. The whole class would burst into laughter as soon as we entered the room. I cursed them all and wiped the blackboard clean with a duster. The class took this opportunity to chorus 'nalla ali,' punning on 'nalla azhi,' which meant, 'Wipe the board well.'

This type of torment was a regular occurrence. Once, while removing one insult or another, I flung the duster in sheer frustration and digust, hitting the Natural Science teacher. He tweaked my ear and made me scrape my knees on the floor.

I had to grin and bear it. What else could I do, if this was my destiny?

The constant ridicule made school intolerable, and soon it became impossible to walk on the street as well. I was now completely alone. To make matters worse, Manju got married and moved out, pushing me deeper into solitude.

Me and my loneliness—all the company I had. Chithi's daughter, my sister Prabha, was my only consolation.

Since my childhood I had been cuddled and petted by everyone. My little sister was my first experience of petting a child. Playing with her, teasing her and mock-fights with her soon became my favourite pastimes.

When I was in the twelfth, we heard that someone had bought the poramboke land on which our house and the other dwellings of Bhupesh Gupta Nagar stood. The new buyer came to our street and staked his claim to our land. People who had been living there for twenty years were in no mood to vacate— they started an agitation.

As a consequence of the struggle, we were allotted land afresh in an area called Uyyakondan Tirumalai.

While waiting for our new house to be constructed, we rented a house at Somarasampettai for a year.

My boyhood obsession with film heroines and my secret pleasure in cross-dressing to look like them intensified at this point rather than being reduced. I was seventeen—no amount of teasing had any ability to make me behave differently by then. On the contrary, I began to comfort myself that my detractors were only poking fun at my effeminate ways because I felt like a woman inside—because I wanted to be a woman.

I was growing up to be an intelligent young person. Approaching the issue in a smarter way than before, I realized that wearing obviously feminine clothes was a problem.

The solution lay in unisex clothes. Combinations like kurtas or other neutral tops and jeans were common to both sexes, so I started wearing such outfits. Watching film stars like Meena, Roja, Nagma and Rambha prattle away sweetly at TV interviews became a singular delight for me, and I mentally rehearsed play-acting as these stars.

A river ran close to our home at Somarasampettai, in which I regularly bathed and washed clothes at seven in the morning. It was actually no more than a canal, but it was sufficiently deep and clean. On the bank were steps where it was convenient to sit while washing. I enjoyed the quiet solitude of these rituals there on the river bank. The isolation gave me the freedom to indulge my fancies; it awakened my feminine sensibilities enough to make me want to dance. In my imagination, I danced every time I bathed or washed clothes on those steps. Wrapping my towel around me, I swam in the canal and visualized a hero grabbing me in the water.

This is how I met my friend Ilango.

I was generally reserved with men. My innate shyness, coupled with the fear that they might notice my difference and begin to harrass me, kept me aloof for the most part.

Ilango owned a dairy business. Light skinned, he had a bushy moustache, a pleasant smile and dignified good looks. He washed his milk can and his clothes in the river at the same time I went there. I could see him approach the bank from my house.

Initially, I avoided him when he tried to strike up a conversation. I was irritated he was snatching my quiet peace and my freedom, yet Ilango continued to converse with me like a good friend. He mixed freely with me and never made fun of my naïve, effeminate speech; he talked to me about the girl he loved, and the beautiful girls he encountered at bus stops and in buses.

Every time he spoke to me of such things, I was thrilled at the thought of the many men who might enjoy looking at me so.

It made me blush, all right, but I cannot deny those thoughts of mine. As the days progressed, I started wishing Ilango would feast on me the way he enjoyed watching other girls. I became eager to win his love, and started staying at the river until he was ready to leave, bathing long enough to return home with him. On the rare occasions when he was late or did not come to the river at all, I was dejected.

I thought then that what I felt for Ilango was neither love nor lust—Ilango was the man who kindled in me the kind of changes that occur in a woman at different stages of her development.

Ilango was the man who made me feel whole as a woman.

My first friend

My 84% marks in the tenth standard exams may seem impressive, but a comparison with my consistently high performance in previous classes reveals the true state of affairs. Imagine how disappointed my father was with this turn of events, considering how he used to belt me for lacking by one mark when I scored 99%.

Though my father was upset with my poor performance, my marks were good enough to secure admission to the first group in Class XI. My teachers praised my performance, and that helped me escape his wrath.

In the new class, I was no longer the keen student of earlier years. Whether it was a question of lack of interest or one of aptitude deficiency, I was hardly able to concentrate on my studies. There was, building up inside me, an anger: a kind of antagonism towards my father. My innermost thoughts and nature filled with anxiety and fears, I was finding it increasingly difficult to focus on my studies.

As I was struggling to get even 60% marks in my monthly tests, life became torturous every time the mark sheets were handed out. With Appa, it was like going to hell and back each time.

When I managed a mere 74%—well below Appa's expectations—in the public examination, he did what he knew best: he thrashed me black and blue. Did other seventeen-year-olds receive such punishment from their parents?

'What did I do wrong? Didn't I bring you up to study well and take care of this family?' he screamed, even as he rained blows on me. 'Didn't I beg, borrow and steal to educate you? Look at your marks!'

He vented all his frustration and fury on me through stinging blows with his belt.

So far, everything that happened had been as expected, according to the script Appa had perfected—but something no one had expected, something unforgivable also occurred. For years I had suffered Appa's violence without a word of protest—only my screams of pain shattering the surrounding silence. But on that occassion, for the first time, I fought back: I shouted at him and pushed him hard. 'Stop it, Appa!' I yelled right in the midst of his crazed bout of flagellation.

The moment passed. When I saw him stumble and fall, I was at a loss for what to do. I panicked—I snatched one of Chithi's saris and prepared to hang myself from the ceiling fan, but she came rushing in and stopped me. Shock, wailing and the shame of defeat turned the evening into some kind of theatre of the absurd.

Appa was a transformed man after that incident. My unexpected assault stunned him—he could not stomach my newfound aggression. My poor marks had been bad enough, but I had further added injury to insult. He was shattered.

I knew very well that his frequent rages were the result of his love and affection for me, yet I had been unable to contain myself on the day of my outburst, and I couldn't undo the damage.

That was the beginning of a cold war between Appa and me. Even before, I had been scared of coming face to face with him. After that incident, he began to hate any contact with me, and stopped talking to me altogether.

I was changing, too. Gone were my earlier grandiose dreams. At first, I had nursed ambitions of becoming a doctor, giving people injections. Later, I wanted to become the district collector, who distributed electricity among the people. Then, I was consumed by the desire to become a film heroine.

Appa wanted me to apply for admission to an engineering college, but I did not do so. I knew the family would not allow me to study Tamil or English literature, so I opted for computer science. At least I didn't have to study chemistry—a subject I hated.

It was the time IT was coming to the fore, so Appa agreed to my choice. He borrowed money at high interest to pay my fees. There were occasions when his creditors harassed him in public in front of our house—he suffered such indignities for my sake.

I could understand his feelings, his love for me and his dreams. I knew that I had the aptitude for academics; I knew what I could achieve if I paid more attention to my studies. Still, my problem was now dwarfing everything else.

With such strong urges inside me, I could not bear to stay at home. More and more mentally detached by the day, I frequently visited my sister, who lived near the Trichy district collector's office.

Radha already had two children: Indu and Santosh. I was a permanent fixture at her place when the babies were born—weekends found me there looking after the children. The great thing about staying with Radha was that Appa wasn't around to nag me to study. I invariably carried a few books with me while leaving for Radha's house, mainly to impress Appa.

The time I spent with the children was peaceful, but I wasn't comfortable when Mama was around. I thought he was the one relative to see through me and recognize my abnormality, when all the others saw me only as eccentric.

At mealtimes, he always pulled me up for eating like a girl.

'Sit straight, like a man,' he repeatedly said. 'Why do you traipse like a girl, coo like one? Why can't you speak loud and clear like a man?' He made up for Appa's absence! Akka's support was a great consolation. She didn't hesitate to scold me, even spank me when I did something wrong, but she never allowed anyone else to speak a word against me. Though my love for Radha, Indu and Santosh was the reason why I went there often, there was another attraction there as well: Radha's saris. Whenever there was no one at home, I used to close the door, wear one of her saris, watch song and dance sequences on TV and dance. This was something I had been doing from my childhood, and I never missed an opportunity to indulge in this pastime.

I liked to wrap a soft towel around my head and pretend it was my long hair—pretend to be in a shampoo commercial and preen before the mirror, shaking my head this way and that. Sometimes I danced to music I had already recorded—the songs of Chitra, Swarnalata and Anupama. I liked to imitate popular TV anchors standing in front of the mirror, or walk like a fashion model and enjoy my own reflection.

My secret life was the best medicine for my depression, but even that was fraught with risk. I constantly worried about peeping toms and intruders catching me in the act, in fear of Radha's unexpected return, or the children coming back early from school, and terrified that the neighbour, Mallika, would come knocking at the door. Those were pleasant but tension-filled hours.

I took great care to shut all the windows properly, checking and rechecking that I had done so, and then filled the keyhole with paper. Sometimes, Radha or Uncle knocked at the door while I was still dancing. I then took off my sari in a flash and rushed breathlessly to open the door. It is for this reason I always wore a sari from Akka's pile of clothes meant for the laundry: I couldn't fling it away in that manner if I wore a fresh sari, could I? I would have to fold it neatly and put it away, and the delay in opening the door would give the game away!

The freedom, tinged with a little fear, allowed me to visualize myself wholly as a woman. I slung a towel across my chest like a dupatta and revelled in it; I sat leaning against the wall, pulling my folded knees back to my chest, and kept covering myself with the dupatta towel.

I was a girl. Unfortunately, the world saw me as a boy. Inwardly I wanted to be a girl, but I made every effort possible to hide my femininity from the outside world. I took particular trouble to remain inconspicuous at college, the unpleasant memories of my bitter experience at school still fresh in my mind. I lead a false life of strenuous attempts to swagger like a man and speak like one.

College was less trouble than I thought. Starting at 8.30 in the morning, my classes were over by one. From class, I went immediately to the library. I had read the novels of Suba and Rajesh Kumar while at school, and I proceeded to acquaint myself with the writings of Jayakanthan, through his novella, *Rishimoolam*. After that, I started borrowing his books regularly from the library.

The librarians must have been surprised to see so many Jayakanthan novels against the library card of a computer science student, for they began recommending me books to read. I soon moved on to other authors as well—Jayantan, T Janakiraman, Ashokamitran, Anton Chekhov, Mikhail Sholokov, Maxim Gorky and Tanjai Prakash, to name some of them. Some old schoolmates—Ilanchezhian, Leo, Sivasu, Subhash, Kanmani Raja and Vijaykumar—were now in college with me. They were friends who posed no threat to me, and I spent time with them often. Still, I did not get too close to them. Literature and solitude were my companions.

Cultural programmes were held regularly at college and students of all departments participated enthusiastically in them. The only exception was the computer science department, which did not organize any programmes. Undaunted by that, I had selected a short novel by Pramil to perform in the annual college culturals, but my plan remained unfulfilled for want of participation from my coursemates—I needed three actors, and did not have a single volunteer from my department.

During the third year, we were invited to the culturals held by the computer science department of Madurai Kamarajar University. Surprisingly, the head of our department gave us permission to participate. The last one to pass up such an opportunity, I entered my name in the dance competition.

Chezhian, Leo, Sivasu, Prince, Karthik, Subhash and Stalin were the other participants from my department; we started rehearsing strenuously. As the day of the culturals approached, I was overcome by a new anxiety.

I had to share a room with my mates in Madurai. Fear and worry dominated my thoughts, even though they were all boys. In my heart, I knew by then I was not a male, and that made me nervous in their company. All the enthusiasm I felt during rehearsals vanished.

The hosts put us up on the third floor of a building opposite the Raja Muthiah Manram of Madurai, where students from various colleges were staying. All of them were men. My nights became hell, filled with the fear of detection and ridicule by the students gathered there. The same torture I felt in facing such a situation was what had kept me from socializing for much of my life—it was the reason I avoided going to weddings and similar communal occasions.

I decided to grit my teeth and bear it; but Immanuel, a backbencher of my class, was determined to spoil the party for me. He was a huge fellow, who looked like one of those gangsters in movies—someone old enough to be the father of two kids. He was a friend of Karthik, who was taking part in the fashion show included in the culturals. Karthik, Sasikumar and Immanuel formed a group of friends. Karthik was the opposite of Immanuel—a quiet chap, but handsome like the actor Ajith, with a macho gait to boot.

Immanuel's home town was Dindigul—not far from Madurai—and as it was vacation time, he had come to Madurai to witness the culturals. Immanuel enjoyed giving me pinpricks every now and then in class. To him I was just a kid, and in truth, I looked like a schoolboy. He loved teasing me. One evening in Madurai he had evidently been drinking beer, and smelled of it. I spent the night in terror.

I went about spending that fear-filled night by covering myself with my blanket and trying to sleep, while all kinds of thoughts ran through my mind. My friends were chattering around me, discussing women—typically disgusting talk about girls.

'Why do you bring specimens like this guy?' I heard Immanuel ask someone.

Even as I was trying to hide my trembling under my blanket, I heard Leo say, 'Let's leave him alone, mate!' All of a sudden, Immanuel removed my blanket and branded my foot with a lighted cigarette. Some of his mates laughed at me as I got up startled. Leo, Subhash, Sivasu and Chezhian ticked him off.

'Why do you want to harass a kid?' they scolded him. Luckily, Immanuel left me alone after that, but he often poked fun at me in class afterwards, referring to the incident at Madurai.

Soon after I joined college, we moved into our new house at Uyyakkondan Tirumalai. It was no more than a hut, built with borrowed money. We had walls made of thatch. The well to the left of the entrance was filled to the brim and we could collect water with a bucket without so much as having to bend. The first room had a steel cot and a television set, where Chithi and Prabha slept. The inside room was the kitchen—in addition to utensils, it housed a huge wooden box. Beyond a short wall were a cupboard and a bookshelf, with room enough for a person to sleep there, besides. Appa slept in front of the house on a rope cot.

I was no longer scared of Appa; it was my turn to bully Prabha. She was my pet, and I wanted her to study well. Like Radha, she was beautiful, yet she resembled Chithi a lot. I liked to pet her, but also teased her by pinching her cheeks and untying her ribbon just when she was getting ready to go to school.

'Amma, look at him...' she complained to Chithi every time I played pranks on her, reminding me of my old friend Amritavalli.

Prabha usually finished in the top ten of her class in exams. Appa would then exhort her to follow my example and do better. 'Do you know, Saravanan was always first in class?' he asked her every time.

Chithi had changed a lot since she first came home as an innocent sixteen-year-old to shoulder the responsibility of taking care of three youngsters. Giving birth to Prabha within two years and playing their mother's role at Radha and Manju's weddings had made her mature beyond her years.

She was not your typical stepmother, vilified by the world. Far from mistreating us, she was lucky we did not ill-treat her! Of course, Appa made up for that with his military-style dictatorship, his inability to show love. He beat her, too, and she lived in constant fear of him—just like Amma. In time, however, all that changed: Chithi grew in courage and even argued with

Appa as I did.

Those were days I wanted to be like the 'new woman' portrayed in films like *Bhuvana Oru Kelvikuri,* and *Aval Oru Todarkathai*. It was all so complicated: I was a woman trapped in a male body. Physically, I was no woman, but my thought processes when considering my future, my professional career, were those of a woman. I put many of my ideas into Chithi's head, and time and again encouraged her to be bold. Chithi knew nothing of such things as feminism, but slowly learned to voice her feelings.

In surroundings other than home or college, I generally felt quite free to be myself. On such occasions, I walked swaying my hips like a woman, sat with my legs crossed stylishly, or rearranged my hair in a feminine way when the wind blew it across my forehead. I behaved so whenever I felt light at heart. On one such day, I was seated in a bus going from Radha's house back to Uyyakondan Tirumalai, when a man sat next to me.

'Are you from Somarasampettai?' he asked in an ingratiating voice.

'Why do you ask?' I replied with exaggerated irritation. Immediately, I noticed that my companion was different from other men—dark, somewhat plump, about twenty-five, he was someone I'd want to converse with, I felt. In Tamil, there's a saying: one snake knows another.

I realized soon he was like me. His name was Senthil and he was a bank employee. He carried a mobile phone—not yet a common middle class possession—and held a diploma of sorts, I learned. He was a good conversationalist and I liked him. Feeling that I could receive the kind of friendship I needed from him, I took his mobile phone number.

'Isn't it a holiday tomorrow? Shall we go to the Kuzhumayi temple then? We can chat there for a while.'

We agreed to meet at three o'clock the next afternoon. I collected my BSA SLR bicycle from the puncture shop and made my way to the temple. The bicycle I had wheedled out of my sister when I joined college—she was therefore the sponsor of all my rides on it, whether to college or to Radha's house.'I don't want a big cycle like Appa's,' I had told her. 'Please get me a ladies' bicycle.'

The Kuzhumayi temple was a ten-minute bicycle ride from home. There was a bridge on the main road to Puttur. Under the bridge, flanked by dirt tracks, was the Uyyakondan river—well known in the neighbourhood. Once you crossed the bridge you came to another, smaller, narrower, undulating bridge. If you crossed this bridge and followed the rivulet that ran amidst the rocks below, you reached the temple. I parked my bicycle at a convenient spot near the bridge, stood over the water in the middle of it, and gazed at the temple and the river.

The Amman festival at the Kuzhumayi temple was famous for a bloodletting ceremony involving a goat and a chicken. On normal days, the temple is a quiet place, with a handful of devotees present there. The real Uyyakondan river ran behind the temple—it's the water let out through the sluice gate that flows below the bridge. Just beyond the bridge is an ancient banyan tree. The whole place—with its river amidst rocks, its quiet temple and banyan tree—was serenely beautiful.

My bus friend was yet to arrive. Just when I was about to give up, he arrived on a Suzuki motorcycle.

'Sorry, have you been waiting for a long time?' he asked.

'It's OK,' I said.

We stood on the bridge and exchanged information about each other. I was delighted to learn he enjoyed the same secret pastimes that I did.

'Shall we address each other as "dee"?' he asked. Only girls who are close friends use this intimate form of address among themselves. I was in seventh heaven and agreed instantly.

We shared many likes and dislikes—our desires, needs, humiliations, pains and loneliness were all identical. As I talked to 'her', my heart soared with happiness at finding the woman friend I had been seeking all these years. I learned quite a few things from her that day.

I learned of an NGO I could visit where people like us were welcome—many doors would open for us there. No need to regret my short hair any more: I could wear a wig and choose a woman's name for myself. Meeting Senthil was a turning point in my life.

A different world

This was a crucial phase of my life. The reluctant pursuit of my college studies coupled with nervous and exciting forays into my new world through visits to the NGO were a tough balancing act. My BSc Computer Science was now no more than a ritual.

I scored only sixty-one marks in modern art in my degree exams. Appa didn't say anything. He must have prepared himself for disappointments, but he did not stop lamenting my deterioration to Chithi.

'What a waste it's been educating this fellow.'

He became preoccupied with my next course of action in higher education, quite ready to fall at the feet of influential people to find me a seat in MSc or MCA, even though I had told him of my resolve of not doing any such course.

No longer interested in pursuing science studies, I informed Appa that I wanted to pursue an MA in linguistics, shattering his expectations again.

I felt a course in humanities would best suit my involvement in theatre, music, dance and college culturals. My college conducted an annual Tamil festival on a grand scale, including competitions in plays, music and quiz programmes. My friend Prince and I took part as a pair in a literary quiz.

I had won some prizes in similar contests when I was in class ten, but I had never taken all that very seriously. Even though competing after a long gap, it was no surprise when my team won the first prize.

The twelve teams in the quiz contest consisted mostly of arts students. Prince and I, both computer students, proved to be the surprise package among the contestants. The toast of the college, I was bloated with pride when our Tamil professor—who taught us during the second year—complimented me in private.

The day I received the first prize at the Tamil festival, several cultural troupes performed at our college. One of the visiting troupes was Tanthane, run by Gunasekharan—who played a key role in the film *Azhagi*.

I had thought of him as just another actor, but I began to respect him when, to my surprise, the organizers announced that he was a professor of drama. That is when I came to know of the department of drama at Pondicherry University.

I decided that I wanted to join Pondicherry University for my MA, but the problem was that I would then have to stay in a hostel.

Those two days in a boys' hostel in Madurai were bad enough, so I started looking around for other colleges offering a master's degree in drama. The Tamil University at Thanjavur had a drama department, but only offered M.Phil and PhD courses, not an MA. I wanted to join the Tamil University because I could then continue to be a day scholar. This meant I had to look for some other subject—and that's how I decided to take up an MA in linguistics. Appa opposed my choice when I informed him about it, but I managed to prevail over him with my customary stubbornness.

I set out on my bicycle every morning at seven o'clock and reached the train station by 7.45. The train reached Thanjavur junction by 9.15. Taking the narrow path to the right of the railway track instead of the main road on the left, I reached the overbridge. From there I caught a bus to the university quarters bus stop, adjacent the rear entrance of the university.

My classes got over at 4.00 p.m., after which I spent an hour or two at the library or the dramatics department. In the evening I took the 7.30 Mysore Express, reaching Trichy by 8.45, and home by 9.30. My postgraduate studies followed this unfailing routine. It was a relatively trouble-free time for me, and my university days were much happier than my undergraduate years. Absent were the pinpricks and lewd jokes of the past.

Still, one inescapable question was regularly directed at me: 'Why have you chosen linguistics after graduating in computer science?' Even my professors said, 'If you had opted for Tamil literature, you could have hoped to get a teacher's job.'

My dream was to become an actor (actress?), journalist or researcher; it had never occurred to me that I could become a teacher or clerk. Nor was I interested in fulfilling my father's dream of my joining the IAS. I was focused on my studies and pursued linguistics enthusiastically, unfettered by anxieties about my employment prospects.

It is not entirely true to say that I studied with enthusiasm. Though interested in my studies, I spent most of my time on dramatics and could not find enough time for linguistics. All my attention was focused on theatre.

There were six of us in my class—three girls and two boys. The other five had taken linguistics because they could not get into Tamil literature. For all my keen interest in the subject, my attendance was irregular, yet exams were no problem—I managed tests quite well, preparing in the library. A fame of sorts accrued about me in literature and allied fields because of my performance in linguistics seminars, so my poor attendance was forgiven thanks to my image as a good student.

The drama department consisted of an open-air theatre surrounded by a semicircle of four rooms. Seeking to introduce myself to the head of the department, I approached him as he was doing some work at his desk. The professor, simply dressed and white bearded, sat patiently as I spoke. 'Sir, I am a linguistics student. I am very keen on acting in plays. Please give me a chance in one of the plays your department produces.' I pleaded with him.

'Where do you come from, young man?'

While I told him about my background, I looked around the room. There was a strange beauty about it. He was seated behind a large table. In front of it, where I sat, were four chairs. The bookshelf next to him had many encyclopaedias and books on theatre. There were masks lying around, and many stage props arranged about the disorderly yet attractive space. I quite liked the man amid it: Professor Mu Ramaswami, popularly known as Mu Ra. His two assistants, a clerk and a secretary, were away most of the time attending to work in other departments, so he was usually left alone once they finished their daily drama tasks. He never seemed to be bothered by the solitude—he was totally immersed in his work.

I started visiting him regularly—so often, in fact, that I was regularly mistaken for a drama student—and befriended a number of the professor's students: Venkatesh, Karthi—an actor in 'Chithi', a famous TV serial of the time—and John.

Through these friends I also came to know Viji, Ramar and Murugan, of the troupe Othigai Kalai Kuzhu. Thanks to these friendships, I came to play a role in *Samban*, as Samban's ten-year-old son.

None of them had any inkling about my femininity. Or perhaps they knew and did not take it too seriously. Either way, it was a consolation, giving me the comfort and peace of mind to perform without fear or self-consciousness. Among the many books I read on theatre craft and plays at the time, I was particularly impressed by the magic and surrealism I encountered in Murugabhupati's scripts. Coming upon him first in an anthology, he soon became my ideal playwright.

The daily train journey to and from university would resonate throughout my transformations. A student who held a season ticket, I could have never imagined then that I would beg on similar routes one day.

University years were a time of introspection. I thought a great deal about myself and the troubles and woes of my existence. With this warning bell going off inside all the time, I was plagued by the constant fear that people were watching me. Nevertheless, I loved train journeys, window seats and travelling alone. My childhood train journeys to Karur—where Amma's younger sister Meena Chithi lived—returned. When Manju moved to Vadugapatti near Karur after her marriage, I enjoyed the familiar trips to visit her—going from Puttur to the Trichy Rockfort station, and from there to Karur. Trains and train stations had always been a passion of mine.

As a child I went berserk at the station: waiting for the train; watching the track as far as the eye could see; running hither and thither on the platform; sitting on the cement bench and peeping out every now and then to welcome the arriving train. Amma worried constantly that I would get hurt.

'Watch out,' she called after me constantly. Radha had to run up and hold me. Those were enjoyable moments; moments I look back on fondly.

My MA study allowed me to continue my love affair with train travel. My season ticket allowed unlimited trips. Express trains were not out of bounds and I often got into the sleeper compartments. The ticket examiner usually looked the other way, but I still invariably explained that I had gotten into the compartment as the train had started moving. Surely, the train official was tired of this unnecessary explanation!

There was this group of season-ticket travellers—my gang—who rode in the same compartment. One of them was a forty-something, light skinned, plump government official. A second government officer was close to thirty, and there were a couple of young men working in the private sector. And then there was Revati.

Revati was a year older than me. She had qualified for a government job through the Tamil Nadu Public Service exams. Junior Assistant in a government department, she was an avid reader, reading almost solely work-related, exam-oriented material, with an eye on promotion. We became friends thanks to our common interest in books, though my own reading on the train consisted of novels. Every morning at seven o'clock she left Alliturai for Puttur station and travelled to Trichy junction to reach her office, finally returning home by 10.00 p.m.

Revati was someone who satisfied my yearning for friendship with another woman. While my gang did not realize I was a woman at heart, they saw me as a quiet innocent, and began to imagine a different dimension to my innocent friendship with Revati. When they started commenting on the relationship, I began to avoid their company—and Revati. Why should I cause her any embarrassment?

I visited the NGO Senthil introduced me to more often than he did. Many of my ilk were regular visitors there: in public, they were men who wore men's clothes, yet perhaps effeminate in appearance and gait; inside the premises of the NGO, they indulged in girl talk, addressing each other with familiarity as women. In their conversations, they suffixed 'dee'—the form of address Tamil girls use for each other—to their remarks.

Senthil had sounded a note of caution before he brought me to the place. 'It's all very well for you to go there regularly,' he said, 'but make sure people don't find out you are a female. Don't go there too often.'

'Why? Aren't they all like us?'

'That may be true, but most of them are uneducated. When they go out, they exhibit their femininity quite openly. If you get too close to them, people will tease you too.'

God, not that! I did not want to face all that!

The NGO was on a street near the Dinabhumi office. I was on familiar ground at Dinabhumi, where I had done a two-month stint as a part-time proofreader during my final undergrad year. My workplace was on the first floor and the press was downstairs. Soon after I joined, a couple of guys from the layout section and a boy younger than me who worked in the press began to make fun of me at every opportunity. 'Hi, Rambha, hey Rambha,' they often called after me. After enough of this, I grew to dislike working there.

Every time I passed the office, I panicked, worried that one of them would spot and harass me. Scared of the embarrassment of being discovered in the act of visiting the NGO, I was a bit aloof with my 'female' friends there.

Ratnavel was a handsome young man—until his feminine gait and mannerisms gave the game away. When he lisped and cooed with a generous sprinkling of 'podi' and 'vadi' (as girls address their close friends), he really shocked onlookers.

Babu was tall and dark. He wore tight jeans and tight T-shirts and walked like a female model on the ramp. She had done an MA at the Jamal Mohammad College in Tiruchi.

Sneha refused to reveal her male name to anyone. She swayed her hips provocatively, making herself obvious.

These three were regular visitors to the NGO; all three

were men with female tendencies.

The peanut vendor Suresh joined them occasionally. Clad in a lungi, which he hitched up, he briskly pushed his cart around during business hours. The moment he entered the NGO, he was a transformed person, mentally changing into a girl.

'Hey, what's up, girls? Are you all right? Sneha, when did you come?' he would ask as soon as he entered, gesticulating like a woman, giving each of us some peanuts. The moment he went out he was back to being Suresh.

At the NGO, I regularly met people like me who went around in male garb but were women in spirit and urges—known as kothis. There were also those who openly wore women's clothes and looked feminine, some of whom had even undergone the sex change operation. These were known as tirunangais.

Shalini was a tirunangai. She had changed her sex. A specialist in karagattam—a type of folk dance—she liked to dance to film songs. Short in stature, she wore little make-up and liked to ruffle her hair to show off her tresses. The more I looked at her, the more I wanted be like her.

Puja was tall and on the heavy side. Unlike Shalini, she had a stern expression on her face. She, too, was a tirunangai.

Ayesha's complexion was lighter than the other two. She looked like a beautiful girl. No one liked her very much, as she was arrogant about her looks. Still, everyone was jealous of her and I was no exception.

The three were good friends, and had been so from the time they did their post-graduate studies. Having crossed many hurdles together after running away from home, they remained good friends, and had found peace now in their decision to be tirunangais.

The NGO once took us to Bengaluru to participate in a rally organized by a sister NGO there. Babu, Sneha, Ratnavel, myself and some others in masculine clothes, along with tirunangais like Shalini, Puja, Ayesha and a couple of forty-year-olds—Pazhaniammal and Malaysia—were among the travellers on that trip. The journey and the rally helped me make some good decisions regarding my life.

Hundreds of kothis and tirunangais took part in that event. They came from Chennai, Pondicherry, Vizhuppuram, Karur, Erode, Madurai, Namakkal, Hyderabad, Bengaluru and many other places. That day, I came face to face with the distinct world of tirunangais. The experience provided practical knowledge of the many problems confronting tirunangais, beyond leg-pulling and teasing.

In the midst of all that, I did not reveal my true self to any of the participants—Senthil's advice and my fear of being teased made sure of that.

Whenever my friends probed me, I claimed to be on a visit researching kothis and tirunangais. When I went out with them I controlled myself enough to act like a man.

When I could not consistently fool the world, how could I hope to fool my friends? Recognizing the involuntary cracks in my armour, they questioned me, and I stoutly denied all queries concerning studies, family and social disapproval. The pretence could not hold for long.

A time for farewells

Returning from Bengaluru, my mind was in turmoil. My greater interest in theatre, poetry readings and seminars overshadowed my studies, which meant that I had more or less stopped attending classes. I only studied during my two-week long study holidays and the four days of my exams. Even so, I worked very hard.

Tamil University only offered master's courses in literature, linguistics, philosophy, sculpture and archaeology. Each course had about forty students, with the semester exams held in one hall for all the courses. I normally finished a three-hour paper in an hour-and-a-half, watched by all the other students as I dashed out to start preparing for the next day's paper.

Those were happy days for me, free from teasing and harassment. I was in search of my self, going beyond my confusion over my gender. Other elements that made my life relatively comfortable were three close friends among the girls in my class and the fact that my classmates had not discovered my femininity.

Some of my friends in the literature class asked me why I didn't mix with the boys in my section. I fielded such questions with a smile. They probably thought I avoided empty chatter for fear of losing focus on my studies.

Unfortunately, I didn't enjoy similar immunity from ridicule on the train. When friends made cheap comments about my friendship with Revati, the episode affected me badly.

I had no problem with people recognizing my femininity, but hated it when they made fun of me on that account. Worse was when they imagined I was a man sexually or romantically interested in a woman. I could not bear comments that involved a girl in such a manner. To you, I may seem to be a man, but I am a woman at heart. How can I tolerate any suggestion that I am in love with a woman?

My experience in dramatics, with its friendships and networking, saved me. Mu Ramaswami had written a play and started casting for it. Rehearsals were about to begin at Madurai and Ramaswami had asked 'Rehearsal' Viji to scout for one new actor. My friend and I attached ourselves to Viji, in the hope of at least watching the rehearsals, but when we reached we found the role had been taken. The professor, however, did not have the heart to turn us away, so he asked us to work backstage.

During the ten days of rehearsals, Ramaswami and his PhD scholars camped there for the entire period. They all lived for theatre; there were playwrights, actors and other experienced artists among them.

The play was staged at the Yadava College for Men, Madurai. A whole lot of research scholars training under Mu Ramaswami; the professor himself; veteran theatre persons like Azhi Venkatesh, Kartikeyan, Pazhani, Maharasan, Professor Govindaswami, Tamil professor Shahjahan Gani; three Tamil students from Thanjavur University; my mates from Thanjavur—Vijay, Ramar and I: all of us camped there for the ten days of rehearsal and the day of the play. Everyone in the group was wholly committed to theatre. And every one of them was a man.

The play, which had no female parts, was called *Agitator Comrade Periyar*. No girl, in fact, contributed to the play in any way—except me! Those ten days in the sole company of men were not as bad as my college days.

It wasn't a make-believe kind of play, but was realistic, a true story. Mu Ramaswami was propagating the Nija Nataka Iyakkam, or Real Theatre Movement. It was drama school that disabused me of the notion that acting meant film acting.

A newcomer arrived within a day or two of the start of rehearsals. Of medium height, he carried a colourful cloth bag and a flute. He looked every bit an artist, with his face reflecting both a childlike quality and passion.

'Who's this man?' I asked Viji, who had been exchanging pleasantries with him.

'Don't tell me you don't know him! He's Murugabhupati, the man you've been wanting to meet.'

I approached him wonderstruck, and hesitantly introduced myself.

'Anna, I've read a collection of your plays. You took me to a surreal world, even if I didn't understand all of it,' I told him.

That's when I met Selvam, a friend of Murugabhupati. Selvam ran a parallel film society for children, called Kunnan Kunnan Kur. I was already moving away from commercial cinema in my tastes, but meeting Selvam introduced me to good cinema. In addition to Selvam and Murugabhupati, I met a number of important persons from theatre and literature during the production.

I made myself useful in many ways, helping at rehearsals as a prompter, as a lighting or stage management assistant, learning useful lessons along the way. The Periyar play experience was a great blessing.

When the play was performed again, incorporating many innovations, I had a part to play in all that. It included Periyar's voice-over, as well as some projected visuals of him, and I was in charge of the audiovisual part of the play. Most of the time I was clumsy, but it was all a learning experience.

It was also my responsibility to arrange for mock questions to be asked from the audience, as well as to personally ascend the stage with a couple of others towards the end of the performance in the guise of TV journalists. I used the opportunity to imitate the diction and mannerisms of a well-known female TV anchor.

Once, Murugabhupati stared at me for a while and said, 'Your face has a certain art about it that is a mixture of male and female.'

I was stunned. He was a born artist, the grandson of that theatre expert Madhurakavi Bhaskaradas, and brother of writers Konangi and Tamilselvan. The intuitive vision of such an accomplished artist moved me deeply. I felt a strong urge to kneel before him and pour my heart out, weep wordlessly, cathartically. While I did nothing of the sort, to recall his words repeatedly was an ecstatic experience.

Throughout the production I had to share the room with many men, shower in communal stalls—minor irritants.

Besides the Nija Natakam group, I also worked with another group, called Karmugil Kalaikoodam, at Tiruchi for a while. It was for a play directed by Muthuvel Azhagan, Melanmai Ponnusami's successor. Called *The 18th Battle*, it was about the eighteenth day of the Mahabharata War, when Aravan, son of Arjuna and snake-maiden Ulupi, succumbs to Krishna's trickery on the battlefield. Aware from birth that he would never inherit his father's legacy, which was reserved for Abhimanyu, and denied Arjuna's parental protection all along, Aravan is a bitter, angry young man. He is also made the scapegoat of the Pandavas in their search for victory in battle. The night before his death, he is seduced by Krishna in the guise of Mohini who becomes his wife. When he dies, Krishna as Mohini mourns his death in the traditional oppari or mourning singer mode.

My friend Senthil, who runs a literary magazine now in Tiruchi, also acted in the play. We performed the roles of narrators. Every now and then some onlookers would tease me during rehearsals when my femininity came out without my knowledge. Once, I had lost myself before the mirror in admiration after the make-up artist had put lipstick on me when Senthil came into the green room. The mirror may reflect your outer appearance to you and others like you, but in the case of tirunangais it portrays their innermost feelings and turbulence, their essential femininity, displaying all. Other people cannot understand this phenomenon. Your face may be mirrored when you sit before a dressing table, but in the case of people like me, our hearts are as clearly mirrored. When Senthil came into the room, I was self-forgetfully drinking in my own beauty as reflected by the mirror, encouraged by my solitude.

In that instant, he must have received confirmation of what he had already suspected. He stood quite stunned, but quickly recovered. 'Ennadee, Saravani,' he teased me, without malice. Embarrassed, I made some pleasant noises and walked away.

After that first show of *Agitator Comrade Periyar*, we performed some forty shows over the next two years at centres such as Chennai, Madurai, Namakkal, Erode, Tiruchi, Coimbatore, Salem, Teni, Bodinayakkanur, Thanjavur, Tiruvannamalai and Pondicherry. I took part in every show.

All the members of the troupe became my friends. On one occasion I acted like a girl for the benefit of Maharasan and a couple of other university students. Actually, I was pretending to imitate a girl for fun, and they liked my 'acting'—but deep inside I was not really acting; I was subtly expressing my inner urges.

This became a regular routine during rehearsals, and they started addressing me playfully as 'dee' all the time.

In a short while they realized I was not acting. What they saw, they discovered, was the truth. At first they were shocked, and after a while they began teasing me constantly. It hurt me a lot.

In the midst of all the dramatic activity, the frequency of my visits to the Tiruchi NGO increased. I enjoyed my sojourns there as a tirunangai and a kothi more and more. Eventually I moved beyond the NGO and started frequenting bus stands, where tirunangais gathered in numbers. Spending time with them became a pleasurable activity. In the beginning I tried to hide my sexuality, but after a while I began to roam around in my trousers as a kothi.

The kothis and tirunangais roaming around bus stations were looking for sex work. They had no other livelihood. Therefore, it wasn't easy for them to spend time with me and entertain my beginner's curiosity and excitement at meeting my kind of people, for, every moment spent with me meant loss of business.

There are always people who poke fun at us, calling us 'Alis'. Many of these approach tirunangais with sexual intent.

I watched everything closely. It is difficult to describe the flaming desire inside me at that time to parade as a tirunangai before all those who had teased and harassed me. Wanting to walk tall in my new identity, I strutted around the bus stand swaying my hips.

This was a reaction—an overreaction maybe. What I had feared would be exposed all these years, I was now dying to express. My age, experience and maturity were directing me to such a state. Sometimes men followed me when I walked around that way. I liked leading them on and then disappearing from the scene, enjoying this cruel revenge on a society that had revelled in teasing me for my effeminacy.

Time flew, what with my involvement in theatre and literature and my friendship with tirunangais. I wrote the MA exams. When the results came out, I learnt I had finished first in the university. There were only six students, but it was still no joke to come first. Unfortunately, I could not celebrate my success.

Pursuing doctoral studies in dramatics had been my ambition during my MA, but now my femininity was growing more intense by the day. I was quite unsettled by the fiery conflict within me; a conflict I was unable to comprehend. There were several choices before me: one, I wanted to be a theatre person; two, I was obliged to take up a job of my father's choice; three, and most importantly, my most virulent desire of all, my urge to follow my natural inclination to break free of the maleness I had been born with and be a woman.

I worried most about my father. He had borrowed money at high interest to educate me, and I was destroying his dreams one by one. He was already a defeated man.

How could I tell him I was not Saravanan, but a girl? How would my loving Chithi, my elder sisters whom I loved more than my life, my younger sister who it seems had been born to shower me with her love, how would they bear the shock of my disclosure?

I had made many friends at the NGO, many kothis and tirunangais, but none of them could guide me. Sri came into my life at the right time.

Sri is a kothi like me, a kothi whose thought processes match mine. He had a master's degree in computer science and was working in a private sector IT company. He held a good job and came from a well-off family in Madurai, now settled in Chennai. He was the youngest son, and faced the same kind of social and family problems as I did.

'I worked hard at my studies,' he told me. 'Today, I don't care about anyone's criticism. I do my duty towards my family. I also have the time and freedom to visit the NGO. I go to

Koovagam annually to attend the congregation of people like us.'

He said all this to console me when we were both seated on a bench at the bus station opposite the Tiruchi railway junction, as I laid my problems before him amidst sobs.

'Don't ever give up your studies,' he advised me. 'Go to Koovagam once a year and take part in the festivities there as a woman to your heart's content. Spend time periodically with the NGO, and take part in festivals and celebrations. But never stop studying. Complete your PhD, earn a good salary, be a good son to your family. Act in plays if you like. Find expression for your desires in privacy. That will be good for you and your family. But if you are adamant about undergoing sex change, you will end up a beggar at these very same bus stands. Can you do it? You are well educated. You'll never be able to do it.'

Everything he said was true, but I could not lead a double life any longer.

No, I couldn't live any longer as a man. If I could not become a woman, I'd rather die. I wasn't confused now. I had come to a clear decision, and it burst out in words. Suicide had been an option in my mind over the last few days.

I buried my head in Sri's lap and broke into sobs. My decision was firm, bold. I hated being a man. I was going to try and live as a woman. If I failed, I was ready to die.

The same night I went to Nehru's house. He was a friend I knew from the time I worked at Karmugil Kalai Koodam. He was in the film industry, an assistant director in many films, and a person I respected greatly.

I went into the narrow street where he lived and rang his doorbell. A dog barked. Nehru opened the door. 'What are you doing here at this hour?'

I was too choked by impending tears to speak. He understood my predicament and invited me in. He waited for me to have a good, long cry. Then he gave me some water to drink.

'Now tell me. What's the problem?'

'Don't ask me why, Nehru, but please help me get a job at once in Chennai.'

Nehru showed his customary maturity. 'Done,' he said, and waited for me to speak on.

'Nehru, I must tell you something,' I began. 'I don't know how you will take it, but please, please, don't give me advice.' I was confident he would understand me.

Still, I went into a long preamble. I just poured out all that I had bottled up inside me for so long, not giving Nehru a chance to get a word in edgeways.

Nehru was shocked, contrary to my expectations. Initially quiet, he started advising me once I came to. 'Don't play with fire,' he told me. 'What do you lack here? Why do you want to court trouble?'

In the end he gave up arguing with me and promised to find a job for me in Chennai.

It was decided I would go to Chennai with his friend Kumaran after a couple of days. He would try to fix me up with a job and introduce me to a good NGO for tirunangais.

When I said goodbye and thanked him, he embraced me and kissed my forehead with pure love and concern.

I came home at four in the morning. Appa was asleep in the open. When I went to knock on the door, I found it ajar, so I gently pushed it, went in and fell asleep, exhausted from all the crying.

I woke up at seven o'clock.

'Chithi, I'm off to Chennai tomorrow,' I announced. 'I have got a job there. I'll be moving there permanently.' Such travel announcements, even if only for a few days, I addressed to Chithi rather than Appa.

'Bye, Appa; bye, Chithi.' I shouted my farewells every time.

While packing clothes and preparing for the journey, my inner voice said, 'Why do you pack these men's clothes? You won't need them any more.'

I was to meet Nehru at five o'clock at his place, so I left the house at 3.30, before anyone in the family came home. Prabha was expected back from school at four, Chithi around five, and Appa could come back any time. Avoiding them all, I picked up my suitcase and walked out briskly.

When I had gone some distance, a TVS 50 passed me and then turned back—it was Appa! Anxious to come back before I left, he had taken a ride from a friend.

Afraid he would stop me, I didn't give him a chance to speak. 'Bye, Appa,' I said immediately.

I had never seen Appa in such a pathetic state. A close look at him revealed tears in his eyes. It was as if he knew in that instant that his beloved son's journey was the precursor of a huge shock.

'Are you really going, Saravana?'

Words failed me altogether. I nodded silently, and walked away from him as fast as I could.

A new path, a new journey

My first task on arriving in Chennai was to try and find a place to stay. The target was a room in one of those so-called 'mansions'—large, usually multi-storeyed buildings, with several rooms let out to bachelors working in the city. These are really tenements, offering varying degrees of comfort. They are generally affordable and well-located.

Kumaran and I went straight from the station to the seaside locality of Triplicane, at the heart of town, in search of a mansion. We went to several mansions in that crowded neighbourhood; me carrying a suitcase in my hand and much confusion in my head.

Rooms were available in almost every mansion, but most of them were on the third or fourth floor. I was breathless by the time I finished climbing those stairs, but Kumaran, who had earlier stayed in a mansion, scaled them effortlessly. Finally, we found a good room on the street adjacent to the rear passage of the Devi cinema complex on Mount Road. Kumaran and I shared the fairly comfortable third floor room.

Kumaran couldn't believe I was a tirunangai. He could not accept that I was a girl. Not due to leave for Chennai for another week, he had advanced his trip for my sake, accompanying me only because his close friend Nehru had asked him to.

I hadn't slept for two days. Bus travel didn't agree with

me, and I had been unable to sleep on the way to Chennai. As much as I loved trains, I disliked buses—I hated the noise, the speed, the pollution and the honking.

We had travelled by an especially noisy, decrepit old bus. On the way to Chennai, I explained my problems to Kumaran, adding to my exhaustion. I crashed to sleep in the room as soon as we entered it.

Kumaran went to sleep as well. Once he woke up, he went out to bring us both some lunch. After lunch, I asked him if he would take me to the beach later. He said, yes, he would. The beach was just a ten-minute walk from our room.

We went to the beach that evening, walking past the Press Club on Wallajah Road. He pointed out the MA Chidambaram Stadium at the Chepauk cricket ground. 'This is Madras University,' he pointed out later. I sighed—Madras University was one of the four universities in the state to offer linguistics— and moved on in the disappointment that accompanies the loss of something dear.

On the beach, amidst the breeze and the waves, Kumaran narrated his experiences in Chennai. I watched the buzz all around me with wonder.

Next day, Kumaran took me to SWAM, an NGO for kothis in male garb. We took a suburban train to Saidapet station and walked from there. We had to search for quite a while before Kumaran could locate the place, which, when we reached we found was closed on Sundays.

Next morning, I went there again. I was hoping to find a job there, so that I could spend time with friends like me, thinking I could be a full time kothi, working there and staying with a fellow kothi. What I found there instead was advice, from an Anglo Indian, among others.

'Why do you want to stay here permanently? Don't ruin

your life by undergoing sex change. With your education, you can get a job elsewhere and visit this place to enjoy the company of fellow kothis.' This was the constant refrain those days.

I realized this was not the place for me. When I was about to leave, a kothi around my age joined us. 'Who's this girl?' she asked, before introducing herself. Her name was Jyoti.

Neutral name, I thought. With a name like that, she could pass herself off both as a man and a woman. She had her hair coloured and wore an earring in the shape of a bindi.

'My name is Preeti,' I told her. I never mentioned my male name to anyone there; Sri had advised me never to reveal it to kothis.

'They will constantly tease you with your man's name if you do,' he had warned.

'So, your name is Preeti,' Kumaran teased me on the way back.

'Yes,' I said, in my best feminine manner.

I liked the Hindi film actress Preity Zinta. A beautiful girl, energetic and sprightly, she was then in Mani Ratnam's film, *Uyire*.

Before Preity Zinta I was a fan of Sushmita Sen, but I unfortunately knew a kothi by the name of Sushmita in Tiruchi, and so had ruled that name out for myself.

It was a happy day, and well spent. Even if I did not find a job there, I met many fellow kothis at SWAM, and that gave me much comfort. At night, I asked Kumaran how he knew about the NGO. He said he had come to know about it while doing a survey in the course of his work.

I got on well with Kumaran. The only problem I had with him was his smoking habit. We kept our windows closed to avoid mosquitoes, so I had to manage to sleep somehow in the midst of cigarette smoke.

Next morning, Kumaran said he was taking me to a couple of places.

'Where?'

'Just come with me. You'll know.'

We took a train to Nungambakkam. From there, we walked to Choolaimedu, where we approached THAA, an NGO. The office had not opened yet. We met a girl student who was there to conduct a survey of tirunangais. We spoke to her and a woman official. Soon, a number of tirunangais arrived there. One of the tirunangais working in the office had long, thick hair, a dark complexion and chiselled features.

Back in Tiruchi, Sri had mentioned some important tirunangais in Chennai—Dhanamma and Neelamma in particular. Both of them came to THAA while I was there. They were both pleasant and friendly enough.

'Do you want to stay with us?' they said. 'We'll take good care of you.'

I did not reply. I had heard unsavoury things about Neelamma, and was quite scared of them both.

Sri had told me Neelamma was one of the most difficult people in Chennai. She was always itching for a fight and no one could hope to win a war of words with her. Sri had given me much useful dope on a number of other tirunangais in the city, too. I'd remembered Neela's name in particular because I had a neighbour with her name back in Puttur.

She wasn't so bad, though, and was quite friendly with me. Time flew as I chatted with Neelamma and Dhanamma; so much so that I forgot Kumaran had accompanied me. He sat waiting wearily nearby.

In a while, the director of the NGO, Ashabharati, joined us. I told her all my problems.

Ashabharati gave me the same advice everyone had given

me so far. She stressed the importance of education and warned me about social disapproval. 'You are a man, remain a man,' repeating what everyone had told me so far.

I was sick and tired of it. I decided it was wiser on my part to wait for realization to dawn on people than try to convince them now of the significance of my feelings and aspirations.

During the conversation, Ashabharati showed me a feature story on her carried by a magazine called *Puthiya Katru* (New Wind). Pleased to note that Mu Ramaswami had written it, I told Ashabharati I had worked with Ramaswami in theatre for two years. 'Sir knows me well.'

'Not bad! You've acted in theatre! Why then do you want to take all this trouble? Why don't you continue to act and study further?'

I was puzzled. Wasn't she a woman like me? Why then was she advising me to continue to be a man? This was no casual interest like my foray into theatre. This was my need: my existence; my very survival. I was a woman, not a man. Why couldn't they understand that? What foolishness! How annoying!

Kumaran came to a decision. 'Look,' he told me, 'no one is taking you seriously. None of them will help you. Why don't you take a job that I find for you now? Come here during weekends and spend time with your friends. That seems the best course of action.'

He took me to an office in the same part of Choolaimedu, a few streets from THAA. The managing director of the company met us after a few minutes of waiting. It was a company run by a couple, doing surveys for large business houses. The company helped its clients with test marketing their products.

At Kumaran's request, the company interviewed me quickly and recruited me to do surveys for them. I underwent a briefing and training programme and was allotted a particular area as my beat, one among many others who fanned out across the city. I left them agreeing to join the next day.

On the way back, I called Professor Mu Ramaswami. He immediately recognized my name and asked me when I moved to Chennai. We exchanged the usual niceties and then the conversation moved on to other generalities. I was keen on confiding in the professor, expecting him to understand my problem. I knew I couldn't bring myself to tell my father I wanted to be a woman, but it was time, I thought, to tell this father figure.

After much hesitation, I mentioned an article I had read by him in *Puthiya Katru*. Then I said, 'I must tell you something.'

'Go ahead.'

'Sir.'

'Don't hesitate, Saravanan.'

I was close to tears. I remembered Appa and thought of my PhD ambitions.

'Sir, I am one of those.'

'What's that?'

'I am like Ashabharati?'

'What does that mean?'

'Sir, I want to change my sex to a woman's. That's why I came to Chennai.'

After a stunned silence, he said, 'What are you saying?'

'Yes, sir, it's true. I want to be a woman. I can't be a man any more. My whole life is a lie. I don't know why, but I wanted to tell you. That's why I called.'

'What's all this, Saravanan? I don't understand you at all. Just work hard and concentrate on your PhD. You'll have no problem then. You can see about sex change after that.'

'No, sir. I can't wait. I want to live as a woman. Nothing else seems important now.'

Ramaswami gave me a lot of advice. He tried to cheer me up, too. I cried and wept and hung up. In a way, crying helped lighten my burden.

I started work next morning, covering a different area each day—Mylapore, Triplicane, Royapettah, Chetpet, Saidapet and so on. I had to take buses everywhere. My office prepared me thoroughly with a route map and bus service details.

My first survey was on behalf of a computer firm. It was a thankless task. You knocked on countless doors, but people rarely cooperated. Even the helpful ones grew tired of the length of the interviews. My target was seven successful calls a day. At half an hour per interview, collecting took half a day. It was usually three in the afternoon by the time I finished. I would then grab a bite somewhere and go to the office. By the time I finished writing the survey report and went home it was evening.

I was paid on a piece rate basis, depending on the number of reports I submitted. Free to do two surveys a day, if I could, I preferred to finish my work early and go to THAA, where I could meet my tirunangai friends and chat with them. Nothing was more important to me.

One day I went to Neelamma's house, and to the house of Sankariamma, who I met there. I was happy to see how happy they were, living the life of their choice, even if it was a constant struggle to assert their femininity. How many challenges they must face every day in their open choice of womanhood!

When I compared myself with them, I was disgusted with my double life. It was a humiliating burden. I felt a strong urge to discard my manhood then and there.

'I can't go on any longer, Kumaran. I don't want this double life,' I told him. 'I want to be a woman. Please understand me, Kumaran. I want to be a woman, even if it means begging on the streets,' I said weeping uncontrollably.

He was shocked. I was overcome by emotion, no doubt, but what I said was the truth. The only way I could live the life of a woman was by beging or becoming a sex worker. Neither my linguistics nor theatre experience could help me here. Vowing never to be a sex worker, begging was my only option.

Kumaran gave me a lot of advice, trying to change my mind. Nehru spoke to me for hours on the telephone. In my heart, the decision to become a woman had taken firm root, the transformation in my mind and body complete. It was impossible to continue as a man, I explained to both of them. After long arguments, Kumaran seemed to understand me.

Aruna is a tirunangai, whom I had seen in a television interview once, and met during a survey. Kumaran took me to meet her. Aruna was slightly plump, with a nice complexion; she looked very feminine. I liked her instantly. She ran a social service outfit.

Aruna listened to my story patiently. She was very supportive, and accepted me straight away as her daughter.

Her life had been similar to mine. She too was a bright student like me, but dropped out after the tenth, to pursue the life of her choice. She too was the recipient of corporal punishment at her father's hands. She too had faced a great number of obstacles and challenges, and had traversed the same pain, trouble and journey as me.

I stayed with her for two days. When I asked her for a job in her NGO, she said there were no openings there. 'This is an NGO that offers counselling and medical help to kothis,' she told me. 'You have no experience. I advise you to live the life of a tirunangai for a while and learn all about it. I'll find you a job after that.'

What she said made sense. I had decided to become a woman, and so had to plunge into that life. I had to try and beg on the streets. It was time I made such a move. I told Arunamma I had made up my mind, but did not want to beg in Chennai. Could she help me relocate elsewhere? Aruna held my hands with love and concern. Her support meant so much to me. It was a salve for the deep wounds the future would inflict on me.

Aruna decided to send me to Pune, to her 'amma' and my 'nani', Sarada Ammal. Handing over all my men's clothes to Kumaran to give away and entrusting the care of my certificates and mark sheets to him, I gave up my week-old survey job and went to Arunamma's place.

The moment it was decided to send me to Pune, my ear and nose were pierced. When I moved to Chennai, I had already grown my hair long enough to tie in a bun. As all my theatre friends had long hair, my family believed I too had grown my hair long for the same purpose. None of them suspected any other reason.

I used to wear Manju's skirts and Radha's saris inexpertly, in great secrecy. Today, I wore a white sari with blue flowers printed on it that Gautami Amma gave me and helped me put it on. I placed a dot on my forehead, tied my hair in a bun and stood before the mirror. I was a woman—a beautiful woman. I realized I resembled Radha and showed my friends her photograph, so proud I was a woman like Radha.

I called Sri to inform him of my decision to move to Pune. He agreed to meet me in Chennai the next day.

Sri and Kumaran came to meet me at the Nungambakkam railway station. Kumaran was overwhelmed, shocked to see me in a woman's garb. Struggling to call me by name, he didn't utter a word. And Sri was strong. He must have been mentally prepared for the turn of events.

He still made a last ditch effort to persuade me to change my decision. Neelamma also had echoed his advice, as had

Sankariamma. She had even taken me to an NGO in an effort to find me a job there, but it was I who had been impatient.

Sri went a step further. 'Look at me,' he said. 'Am I not a kothi? I am educated, too. I have a steady job. Don't I take time out every now and then to lead a woman's life? Why can't you follow my example? Why do you want to undergo so much suffering?

'With all your qualifications, after all your struggles, do you want to end up a beggar?'

I understood every word, knowing my friends only had my welfare at heart, but I hated to be a man in public and a woman in private. I found wearing men's clothes disgusting. Nobody's advice could shake my resolve. I was a woman and I was nothing without my passion to be a woman. It was more than a passion even: it was an obsession. My womanhood was raging to destroy my manhood, incinerating all the advice I was receiving.

The Chennai Central railway station was choc-a-block with people. There was noise everywhere. In the all-pervasive throng of urgent passengers, I felt I was an island of calm. My heart was filled with joy; it was ecstatic. I was going to be a beggar, but as a woman! Nothing was larger than that. I was no more Saravanan. This physical shape was not me. Preeti!

I asked Kumaran not to come to see me off at the station. When I called Nehru to say goodbye to him, he didn't tire me with more advice, but spoke encouragingly, giving me confidence for the journey ahead. Sri did not turn up at the station.

The Dadar Express sped towards Mumbai, the land of freedom that had since long sheltered tirunangais. I sat entranced by the rhythm of the speeding train, dreaming of Pune, my future home.

Accept me!

Kalaichelvi Ayah took me to Pune by train. According to the tradition of tirunangais, she was my nani, or maternal grandmother. Another 'amma', Shanti, also accompanied us. They spent most of the journey playing cards and bossing over me. They constantly gave me errands to do.

I didn't mind all that, nor did I resent their bossiness. All the struggles of the past to establish my identity as a woman had hardened me. I was imperturbable, prepared to do anything to lose all traces of manliness in me, and thus wholeheartedly embraced the sorority of transgenders.

Older tirunangais usually expect a demonstration of a great deal of respect from younger tirunangais. They demand implicit obedience, and won't tolerate younger girls sitting with them on an equal level. Touching their feet is another standard expectation.

Showing respect to elders is something Indians have come to accept as part of tradition, but the demands made by older tirunangais exceed all these social requirements. One has to carry out every errand without a murmur; even cleaning their spittoons till they shine. Pressing their feet is something they constantly wanted us to do.

My amma in the world of tirunangais was Arunamma,

who ran an NGO and was in contact with the external world. I did not face the usual problems between junior and senior tirunangais with her. Many tirunangais lived in Choolaimedu, where her NGO was located. They often visited us and gave me the kind of troubles Arunamma spared me, but these were brief inconveniences.

Once you settle down in a group of tirunangais, the harassment stops. The arrival of a new tirunangai helps to some extent, as attention is diverted to her. Somewhat in the manner of college ragging, victims turn tormentors overnight. Unlike college students, these are people who have been marginalized by society, insulted and humiliated, even cursed. Perhaps they find some semblance of release from their torments by occasionally taunting others.

I was always of independent spirit, refusing to submit to anyone without reason. Nothing was more important than preserving my dignity. Whether my education or my inherent nature were to blame for this, I am not sure. When Kalaichelvi Ayah and Shanti Amma tried to boss over me and gave me frequent errands, I had to check my pride.

Priya's voice caught my attention. She was going to Pune with us. I had met her once at Aruna's place. She had joined the tirunangai clan when she was sixteen.

At Aruna's place, she had introduced herself, 'My name is Priya. You…?' We were of the same age and she was very pleasant company. I liked her immediately.

Priya was about my height. Clear complexioned, she had a lovely smile. Her simple clothes and make-up benefited her attraction. We hit it off at once.

After a day and a half of travel we reached Pune station—a particularly lovely junction. We took the ramp to the nearby flyover and reached the main road in no time. There was another exit through platform no.1, past the booking office with an ancient banyan tree and a small temple next to it.

We exited by the ramp and reached the auto rickshaw stand.

Kalaichelvi Ayah told the driver, 'Bhaiya, take us to City Post.' I was eagerly watching the sights along the way, trying to learn the route. Kalaichelvi Ayah continued instructing me on how to behave once we reached our destination. 'Don't go wandering around. Follow me closely. As soon as you enter, fall at Nani's feet and receive her blessings.'

City Post is in the heart of Pune, surrounded by busy shopping areas. Several streets criss-cross this area, all of them leading to the main road at different points. The street we were headed for was in the thick of a market area. At the narrow beginning of the street was a public convenience, after which the roadway widened progressively, with houses lining it on either side. Our auto rickshaw reached there in ten minutes.

When the auto stopped, Ayah dragged me by the hand in a tearing hurry. I couldn't even say goodbye to Priya. To make things worse, she literally ordered me not to loiter aimlessly.

We walked some distance before turning left into a narrow lane, where we came to what seemed to be the rear entrance of a house, from which we were escorted up a wooden staircase to the first floor.

I went straight to Nani, who was in an inner room. True to the instructions I received, I said 'Paanv padti', and fell at her feet to seek her blessings.

Nani was dark complexioned and a little overweight. She looked relaxed and natural and not fearsome as I had anticipated. In that tiny room, she was reclining on a wide cot, from where we could watch the strategically positioned TV set. Facing her bed were two windows, offering a beautiful view of the road. The walls were plastered with pictures of gods and goddesses. One of them was a picture of 'Mata'[1]. The elephant god, Ganesha, and the goddess of wealth, Lakshmi, were also prominent in the display.

After the introductory preliminaries, Nani came to the business at hand. It was as if she was delivering a well-rehearsed speech.

'You can be yourself here, sing and dance to your heart's content, but always be respectful to elders. At the same time, you must get on well with the younger people. Come to me if you need something. Go out with your akka, Satya (she had enlisted her just before me) everyday and 'shop' (the community's slang for seeking alms at shops). You must bring back no less than three hundred rupees every day. You do that and we'll perform your nirvana in precisely six months.'

I listened carefully.

'Say something.'

Taken by surprise, I said, 'All right, Nani.'

Nani was pleased I was educated, but expressed her pride indirectly.

'Don't walk around with a swollen head because you went to college, OK? Whether educated or illiterate, a kothi is a kothi, do you understand?'

'And don't earn a bad name anywhere. Go about your business quietly, unobtrusively. If you get into any mischief despite my advice, remember I can get nasty. OK? '

I nodded in agreement to all her dos and don'ts. She asked

---

[1]Mata is the goddess of tirunangais. According to legend, an enraged queen dismembers her husband who deserts her because he wants to be a woman, in the process converting a kothi into a tirunangai. The queen is herself instantly transformed into Mata, the goddess, whose name every kothi utters repeatedly during nirvana.

me to go to Mumbai in the evening and do a reet.

'Yes, ayah.'

'What's your name?'

'Preeti, ayah.'

'Preeti!' Ayah seemed to be surprised. She asked me to change my name. There had been a Preeti before me. She died young, so the name was considered a bad omen at my new home. Chitramma proposed the name Deivanai, but I didn't like it. It was so old-fashioned. Then Satya akka came to my rescue. She said, 'My name is Satya. Let's call you Vidya. We are sisters and our names will rhyme.'

Vidya. I liked it. Short and sweet: a beautiful, meaningful name.

'Ok, ayah. I'll be Vidya.'

The back of the house was relatively expansive, with a cement floor and a pillar in the middle. The kitchen—a makeshift arrangement really—was open, with a table for a counter, on which was a gas stove with its cylinder below. A steel cupboard contained utensils and vessels, and a small loft held the provisions. Once you crossed this widish space, the house narrowed to a passage leading to three bedrooms, followed by Nani's room. There was a low ceiling and a small attic, with a small opening through an extended stepladder. We climbed the ladder to reach the bedroom for 'shopping' tirunangais—which group included me. The bedroom was equipped with two windows and a clothesline.

The first time I entered the house, it was ten o'clock in the morning, but all the occupants looked as if they had just woken up. The only exception was tall, fair Shilpa, who was at the breakfast table. She resembled the actress Shilpa Shetty. I was to learn later that she was the highest young earner of the house.

'Have you had your nashta?' she asked me.

'Yes, I have.'

She introduced me to Lakshmiammal. One among the older members of the household, she wore a T-shirt and tight jeans like a young girl, which did not suit her at all. She was searching for a suitcase that contained her clothes. We did not speak to each other, except for the standard obeisance on my part. 'Paanv padti,' I said, and she replied with an artificial 'jeete raho'.

Nandiniammal was a dark beauty, smartly dressed in a bright sari. 'Want some tea, darling?' she asked me, and ordered some without waiting for my reply. It was customary for tirunangais to extend hospitality to visiting tirunangais. Offering a cup of tea was more or less mandatory.

Another member of the household was Parimalammal, who was of medium build, and looked about thirty even though she was closer to forty.

I said 'paanv padti' to all of them and sat down. My sister Satya soon arrived.

Chitramma and Seetamma were the two other tirunangais in the house. They were amazingly similar people, both short-tempered. I was scared of them to start with but got used to them in time.

That evening, Chitramma took me to Mumbai, following Nani's instructions. We reached Kalyan after three hours of train travel, taking an autorickshaw from there to our destination—a house. The atmosphere inside the house was completely confusing.

There was one tirunangai in the house who bore a striking resemblance to the actress Vasundhara Das. She was from Bengaluru but spoke Tamil fluently. After we ate the chappatis she offered us, I cleaned up. As it was past sundown, she suggested we do the reet next morning.

Doing the reet was the term for formally enrolling in the

community of tirunangais. It was a registration procedure of sorts. You paid a nominal sum and you were included in a parivar/parampara list.

A parivar—literally 'family'—is a group. There are seven parivars in Chennai. Each parivar has a name. Examples are Bhendi Bazaar, Punekar and Lalkar. All the tirunangais in Mumbai come under one of these seven parivars. I was registered with the Bhendi Bazaar parivar. A tirunangai wanting a change to a new group has to pay a fine, a kind of transfer fee, to the parivar she is leaving. Usually such transfers follow misunderstandings with the amma or nani.

There is a whole hierarchy of amma, nani, and dadi, i.e., mother, grandmother and great grandmother. Usually, the young tirunangai chooses her amma, and becomes her chela or disciple. She is also named her nani's nathi chela. A senior chela is an elder sister to the relatively junior chela. The mother's sisters become a tirunangai's aunts, the elder one a periyamma and the younger one a chithi.

My reet in the Bhendi Bazaar parivar was registered as Saradammal's nathi chela and Arunammal's chela. After the registration, a veteran tirunangai gifted me a sari. This was again a regular custom. When seniors see off a new tirunangai, or when she goes to see them, the gift of a sari and some cash is mandatory. The life of a tirunangai is bound by thousands of such rules and regulations, all unwritten.

This was three months after I had left home. Life had been on a fast track from Tiruchi to Chennai, from Chennai to Pune, and I was yet to write to my family. I could not call them, as they had no phone at home. God knows how they were coping with the anxiety I had caused them. They must have worried themselves sick, as I did not tell them where I was going.

About a month after I moved to Pune, the great tsunami

tragedy struck several parts of the world, including Chennai—mildly—and other parts of Tamil Nadu. My folks must surely have worried about my fate during the disaster.

Appa, Radha and my Chithi started looking for me. I had long ago given Radha Mu Ramaswami's phone number, so she called him and enquired about me. The professor, who knew my condition, did not know what to tell Radha. He must have been troubled by his role as bearer of bad tidings. After some initial hesitation, he revealed the truth about me to them—that I was a tirunangai, and that I had fled home because of that.

What could have shocked Radha more? It was the most upsetting information she could have ever received—knowledge from which she could not recover. Even if she was able to reconcile herself to the horrible truth of the situation, how could she tell my father?

Appa asked her repeatedly for news of me. 'Do you have any news of Saravanan? How is he? Where is he?' He was tearful and quite shattered. At one point, Radha could no longer take it. She broke down and conveyed my crushing fate to him. I understand what agonies my family must have suffered as a result of my actions, but there was nothing I could do about it.

Once they recovered from the initial shock, and the weeping and wailing was over, they contacted Arunamma through Ashabharati and Mu Ra, from whom they learned that I was living in Pune.

Arunamma summoned me to Chennai. I panicked. How would Appa react to my present state? I had no idea, but I had to face the situation. Appa, your son is a tirunangai. Can you accept me as one, Appa? Akka, you no longer have a brother. You have two sisters, Manju and me. I am Vidya, not Saravanan—Vidya.

I left Pune for Chennai in great turmoil, preparing to meet my family at Arunamma's NGO. They invited my family two days after my arrival in Chennai, and I waited expectantly for Appa and Radha. Radha called me as soon as they landed at the Egmore railway station. They were here!

I prepared myself for the meeting, so distraught that anyone who saw me would have thought I was about to meet an enemy on the battlefield rather than my family. Gathering courage, I went to the station in the company of my tirunangai sisters, Viji and Bhumika.

I wore a beautiful black sari with a broad, silver border. Everytime I wore it, I told myself it would suit my sister better. When I saw Radha at the entrance to the station, my heart nearly stopped and tears filled my eyes.

'Radha,' I called softly.

'Saravana…'

The name sounded so strange, even though it was the name my parents had given me—I was hearing it after such a long gap. Why did my sister call me by that name when I was in a sari?

'Don't call me that. I am Vidya now,' I told her heartlessly. Mama and Sekhar Chitappa joined us. I had not expected Sekhar Chitappa at all. He was a distant relative, a follower of Periyar E.V. Ramaswami Naicker, an aware person. Perhaps the only male relative in whose company I tended to relax, he might have been brought for just that reason. There was no sign of Appa.

'Where's Appa?' I asked Radha.

'He's waiting for you to call him.'

Meeting Radha and Mama was not a major hassle, but meeting Appa was a different proposition. He was certain to break down to pieces. I had destroyed his dreams, demolished his dignity, decimated his pride. How would I face him now?

I went to where he was, not knowing what to do.

'I don't want to see him,' he said. 'Ask him to get away from me.' His last glimmer of hope must have vanished when he saw me in a sari, for his wailing sobs shook Radha, and she started crying, too.

Sekhar Chitappa failed to console Appa as he helped him into an auto. Radha, Sekhar Chitappa and Viji took one autorickshaw, while Appa, Bhumika and Mama took another.

Radha was the first to recover from the shock, maybe because Mu Ra had prepared her for the worst. She must have remembered my childhood fascination with her clothes, or the many times during my college years when I had told her, 'I don't know what's wrong with me, but one day I will wander stark, raving mad, to your surprise and shock.' She remembered as well, perhaps, how she brushed it aside as some juvenile nonsense. Seeming to have understood that I was happy now, leading a life of my choosing, she arrived at some measure of acceptance.

Mama was often sharp with my femininity during my childhood: 'Are you a broad?' he would ask me, annoyed with my odd behaviour—especially when I danced to the voice of Chitra, Swarnalata, Anupama, Vasundhara Das and other female singers. When I enjoyed songs full of the longing, pain, desire and passion of women, he invariably admonished me: 'What kind of songs are these? You have gone and recorded so many.'

Radha gave me a blow by blow account during the ride. She recounted her struggles to break the bad news to Appa, Manju and Chinna Mama; Appa's violent reaction; all the weeping and wailing by one and all; Prabha's incomprehension; Chithi's shock; the terrible impact on other relatives like Periyappa and Periyamma. I couldn't bear to listen to her and cried the whole time.

'Why are you crying? Aren't we the people who must weep? What did you lack? Why have you done this to us?'

Appa refused to see me in a sari. I was equally adamant about not wearing men's clothes. Finally, I wore a shirt I picked out of a bundle of donations to the tsunami victims, deferring to Radha and Arunamma's wishes. Only then did Appa agree to speak with me.

All of us tried to explain my position to Appa, but our attempts were in vain. He was totally unwilling to listen, weeping throughout. The only moment he stopped was to fold his arms and plead with Arunamma to release his son. Arunamma literally wriggled in embarrassment.

I collected my wits and tried to speak calmly to Appa.

'Wouldn't you have accepted me if I had been physically maimed? Why don't you treat my predicament similarly, Appa?' I broke down even as I was saying these words.

Arunamma too spoke to him on my behalf: 'Times have changed. Even science accepts us as we are. We can accomplish what normal men and women can. Please try to understand.'

'Appa, I will prove myself as an actress.' These words made Appa even more angry, and Mama was about to hit me.

Endless discussions brought about no resolution. As day slipped into night, Sekhar Chitappa and Mama took Appa away. They had no choice.

Though I was able to explain my decision to everyone else, I stood before Appa like a criminal. I will always carry the guilt of dismantling his hopes and aspirations. Was I really responsible for his woes?

My worries were mine and his tragedy was his. It was an inconclusive meeting.

The only consolation was that my family now knew the truth.

My world, my people

My situation was no different from that of thousands of other tirunangais. Just like them, I could not live in my own home, with my own family, as I wanted to. How would society view such an arrangement? Good question. What is society? Isn't my society my father, sisters, Chithi and Mama? After all, didn't I live with all of them until I completed my post graduate studies? Even then, I regarded myself as a girl—a woman—though in their eyes I was male. That was wrong. When I demand that they henceforth treat me as a woman, address me as one, interact with me as with a woman, conflict arises; they refuse to accept me as I am. When people cannot accept my gender as I feel it, how can I continue to live with them, even if they are my own people? I can do without constant reminders of their embarrassment, the volcanic eruptions in my father whenever he sees me, the tears he sheds, the curses he directs at me...

I tried to plant a small seed of confidence in my family—even if I was not exactly overflowing with confidence myself.

'Don't worry about me. I am educated and can survive; I am worldly wise and know how to live; I can learn how to live. Yes, I am not Saravanan, but I am a human being, not some monster. Not some demon. My brain will protect me. Bye.'

That should comfort my father a little, I hoped. There was

nothing more I could have done. In a world of men and women, where no one has the maturity to accept us naturally, the place of tirunangais was always going to be a problem. My family is not to blame. They are but representatives of a world of men and women. I had to pursue my path, my life, my desires, my dreams—my future, if I had one. My trail led back to Pune.

Most of the tirunangais from South India migrate to the north, to cities like Mumbai, Pune, Kolkata and Delhi. An important reason for this is that, in these parts, people see them as avatars of Krishna. Either people think it is good to receive their blessings, or fear that their curses could come true. Whether such beliefs are true or false, they have encouraged tirunangais to seek shelter in those cities.

There are some myths and legends about tirunangais in Tamil Nadu, too. For instance, the Pandavas had to offer a sacrifice to Kali to win the war, and elected Arjuna's son, Aravan, for that dubious distinction. Aravan agreed to be their sacrificial lamb, so long as his final wish was granted. Krishna took the form of Mohini and married him the day before his beheading.

Another story from the Mahabharata has Arjuna cursed to take the form of a tirunangai called Brihannala.

In the Ramayana, too, there are tirunangais. They wait for Rama on his return from vanavasa.

Despite their long history, atrocities against tirunangais abound in Tamil Nadu, Karnataka and Andhra Pradesh. Until even a decade ago, no information was available on the extent and forms of such violence in these states. Nobody gave the problem any importance. Most south Indians are god-fearing, religious people, but neither myth nor epic seems to have a positive impact on them where tirunangais are concerned. They don't seem to realize that tirunangais eat, sleep, work hard and live, just like anyone else. People look down on them, approach them in a domineering spirit, with contempt, with disgust, as if very proximity with them could pollute.

What sin have tirunangais committed? If to be born male and feel female is a sin, it is nature's creation. What can we do about it?

It is this negative attitude in South India that drives tirunangais to the northern states. Whether based on faith in Krishnavatara or fear of being cursed, we face fewer problems there. If we want to live as women, and stay clear of violence and atrocities, we have no option but to go north.

Some go to Mumbai, and some to Delhi or Kolkata. I went to Pune, because Arunamma, who adopted me, had connections there. Her 'amma' lived there. Following that tradition, I went to Pune to be nurtured by my 'grandmother.'

I knew life would be no bed of roses in Pune. I knew clearly what I was going to do there—beg, plain and simple. As long as I did not want to be a sex worker, begging was my only option. All tirunangais had to face this cold truth. I prepared myself, and put my MA in linguistics into cold storage.

In tirunangai parlance, begging is very loosely translated as 'shop asking' or 'shopping'—you go asking from shop to shop. The other varieties are 'train begging' and 'traffic signal begging.'

I was sent shop-begging the day after I registered my reet in Mumbai, in the company of Satya Akka. It was an unforgettable first experience.

As I said earlier, there were many rules and regulations governing our lives. One of them mandated that we keep our heads bowed while walking on our home street until we reached the main road. The reason for this was that the street was meant for tirunangai sex workers—only they were allowed to stay there. Also, those who hadn't had their nirvana were normally not allowed to lodge on that road. Those that did manage to be accepted as residents had to follow rigid rules. Thus, I kept my head down close to home.

There were actually separate locations earmarked for the residence of shop-begging tirunangais in Pune. Shivaji Nagar—a prominent slum—was one such locale. None of the houses there had proper walls. Instead, there were four tin sheets on all sides. The roof was also made of tin. Only the floor was different—packed mud. The tirunangais who went out begging at shops were housed in these rented shacks. Very few senior tirunangais among the shop beggars had their own rooms. It was impossible to walk in the area when it rained—the whole place, including the interiors of the shacks, became thoroughly slushy.

A tirunangai could not rent a house anywhere else in Pune for love or money.

My nani Saradamma owned a few such tin properties, so she should have normally put me up in one of those. I don't know what came over her, but I was distinctly lucky, for she accommodated me in the City Post residential area. My sisters Satya and Senbagam (Nandiniamma's chela-daughter) stayed there as well.

My first outing as a shop beggar was to Swar Gate guided by Satya. We took a shared autorickshaw from a market near City Post and passed a series of shopping areas.

'You can't beg in any of these shops, OK?' Satya said to me. 'Not just this bazaar, you can't beg in any of the bazaars around our street. Do you understand?'

'Why, Akka?'

'Don't ask why. You can't—you must not.' Satya was firm. Wasn't she my senior? Though only slightly older than me, she had been part of the tirunangai community for quite a few years now. She constantly reminded one of her seniority in her speech and actions.

The autorickshaw stopped at the Swar Gate traffic signal, where five roads converged. At the end of the wide boulevard was a bridge.

Satya paid the driver and we got off. We reached a bus terminus past the signal. There were people everywhere, and I watched the spectacle wide-eyed—it was all so new to me.

'What are you doing gazing at the crowd? Walk fast,' Satya said. She was from the industrial town of Coimbatore in Tamil Nadu and spoke the local dialect fluently. Her accent made her the butt of many jokes at home.

We approached a row of shops, which resembled a collection of matchboxes arranged side-by-side. The variety was quite impressive—shoe shops, bookstores, teashops, textile showrooms, newspaper kiosks, bakeries, little shops with belts and bags hanging from the roof: a generous assortment.

Satya chose the first shop in each bazaar. For the day's opener she picked a shop where we could get at least a rupee, without any haggling from the shopkeeper. It was a superstition common to shop-beggars that if you drew a blank at the first stop, your day could be a total loss. Moreover, bargaining could lead to disputes, and ruin the whole day—this was only one of many such beliefs in the community.

Satya stopped at the shop she had selected. Clapping her hands, she said, 'Bhaiya, dena! (Give, brother!)' I stood rooted, watching her in action, as though she was seeking a donation and I was her supervisor! 'Come on, stop staring at me. Go to the next shop and start your work!' she told me.

I had butterflies in my stomach. Me, beg at the next shop? I didn't know how to handle the situation. How could she order me to proceed on my own, without any warning?

Of course, I had waited for this moment—it was something I was expected to do, something I now had to. And yet, even as my brain told my hand to reach out, the hand refused to obey! Tears were welling up in my eyes. At that very instant I remembered my MA in linguistics, of all things. I stood there, nervous, hesitant.

'Oh, hell, look at you! Staring like an idiot instead of doing your job! What kind of kothi are you? Your MA doesn't mean a thing here. Come on, hurry up and beg! Let's each go to a different shop. Only then can we collect a decent sum.'

Tirunangais have this highly effective language among themselves. Clapping their hands together is their Morse code. The sharp sound we make clapping our hands can instantly draw the attention of our fellow tirunangais, wherever we are, however crowded the street. Especially in times of need—as in a dispute or quarrel—this mode of communication lends us great moral support. I was still a novice at it.

Satya was fed up with me. 'What kind of kothi are you? Can't even clap your hands.' After my hesitant start, I gradually learned to internalize her style of begging, and imitate her. We started with the row of shops on the left side of the road, crossing intersecting streets, and stopped at every shop along the way. In the afternoon, we covered the shops on the opposite side. Instead of stopping for lunch, we begged for snacks at some of the small teashops, and even managed to get some paan to chew!

Satya Akka took me round to several bazaar areas, to introduce all the target shops to me. There were bazaars full of shops on all four roads in the Swar Gate area, which included the street I visited on my first day. There were three more roads: one adjoining a petrol station, one opposite these two roads, and another beyond the bridge.

Boldigiri Market was a big vegetable market, similar to the farmers' bazaars in Tamil Nadu. Handcarts selling fruits adorn its entrance. The market itself consists of a large circle of shops with smaller circles inside it full of rows of independent stores punctuated with pavement stalls. The first floors were offices. You could spend a whole day begging in Boldigiri. Vegetables and fruits were a bonus, over and above the money you could collect—we carried bags to fill with these goodies, known or unknown to the shopkeepers.

We also clapped at autorickshaw drivers, and many of them gave us money—one rupee per autorickshaw!

Often we took a bus from the Swar Gate bus stand to a place called Sivapur—a beautiful, hilly village, an hour's bus ride from Pune. It was like any other hill station, not different from Ooty or Kodaikanal. It was cold there even during the day, when we went round begging at the local shops. On the highway leading to the village were several stores and restaurants, big and small. Sivapur also had a large bazaar. The shops, unlike those in the other bazaars I knew, were laid out far apart from one another. Beautiful agricultural land separated some of them. The whole scene was pleasant and heartwarming—water gushing out of the pumpsets, wide open spaces, and unpolluted environment.

We finished our daily shop expeditions by around six in the evening. Throughout the day we would exchange our collection for higher denominations of notes. If a shopkeeper was giving me two rupees, for instance, I'd ask for a ten rupee note, and return him eight rupees. We unloaded any remaining loose change at lottery ticket shops and teashops. There were specialist money-changing shops near City Post that charged a commission of five rupees for every hundred! But we mostly avoided paying such commission by changing all our money at smaller establishments.

Within two months, I began to do shops on my own. I started saving enough from the daily commission of fifty rupees to buy myself saris, churidars, bangles, cosmetics and costume jewellery. Having learned quite a few tricks of the trade, I now knew where to start in order to have a successful day; I learned who gave, who did not, who the difficult customers were, who was likely to get into a fight with you, where you had to be tactful and where you had to be a bully—I was becoming an expert, and grew to enjoy my begging trips.

With no specific agenda, I took a break to go to Chennai. For a lark, I tried train begging, though I had gone to Pune in the first place because there was no future begging in Chennai. I realized it was all in the mind. No problem was too big—no challenge too difficult. Nothing was shameful now that I no longer had to hide my identity. Senbagam and Vasanti Ayah were my train partners. Senbagam was my loving sister, closer to me than Satya.

Begging on trains was tougher than bazaars, I discovered. You had to be up at half past six in the morning, shower and be ready by seven. A cold shower at that hour in the Pune chill was not a welcome proposition.

One early morning visitor was an old but energetic ayah who came to scrub our vessels and collect drinking water for us. Despite her age and physical limitations, she rose unfailingly to do these chores, as well as fetch tea and breakfast for all of us. She was brisk and efficient, and her voice reminded me of my paternal grandmother, who worked at a cinema beyond even ninety years of age. Fiercely independent, she cooked for herself, and refused whatever food we sent her. Her steadfast principles were not easy to understand, but she loved me to distraction, especially because I was the first male offspring of her own children.

Vasanti Ayah never ceased to remind me of my grandma. When I got ready and went downstairs at around 7.30 a.m., she invariably answered my call. She did the rounds of train begging until she was fifty, but old age had reduced her to skin and bones. Despite her long years in Pune, she still spoke broken Hindi; quite unclear at the best of times, she raised a laugh when she spoke Hindi, for she murdered the language. Her Hindi was purely functional: '*Arre, dena, kya tum yeh voh bol raha,*' she addressed her victims, demanding alms. Otherwise, she spoke to everyone in Tamil, regardless of whether they were from Kerala, Andhra or Maharashtra. Somehow, she still managed to extract money from them—thanks largely to her elderly appearance and naïve chatter.

Senbagam was also a Hindi-less master of the art of begging. When she said, '*Ye de re, haan,*' in her authoritative tone, people handed over money in sheer fear.

We usually went to Lonavala by the Coimbatore–Lokmanya Express, which arrived between 8.00 to 8.30 a.m., and then took the Hyderabad train up to Khandala. Returning to Pune on the Mumbai–Pune train, we went back to Lonavala by the 3.30 Bengaluru–Mumbai. We took as many as four trains in a day, changing our coins and low denomination notes at the Lonavala ticket counter.

Starting my train saga with Kasturiamma, who was going to her home town, I accompanied her on that journey and begged on the train for the first time. Afterwards, I begged independently on the Hyderabad route, going up to Karjat and catching the train to Sholapur there, also working some local trains. Later, I ganged up with Priya and Prateeksha. Together we begged on my regular route in the morning and the Nagerkoil train in the evening. We did not even spare the shuttle, which stopped at the station in the afternoon.

Priya was the senior in our dol (group), both in age and years of service, but she never held this over us, and we were a happy bunch of alms-seekers on trains. Our cheerful, carefree trio lacked the seriousness of other tirunangai gangs—we were always ribbing and jostling one another. Many rozwalas (regular commuters) were familiar with Priya and Prateeksha, as they had been around for a long time.

Priya's sweet, gregarious nature helped us make friends with not only the rozwalas, but also the ticket clerks, traders and vendors on the platform, the station master, autorickshaw drivers at the stands outside, and almost everyone else connected to the station. In turn, they all became my friends as well.

There were no major problems in my life during those days. It was too good to last forever, though. One fine morning, the leader of the area decreed that no shop-begging tirunangais could stay any longer on that street in the City Post area. In addition to the tirunangais, female sex workers also lived there—a few families did, too. It was declared that tirunangais were only allowed to do sex work if they were good-looking and effeminate. There was also a ceiling imposed on the number of sex workers in each home.

The area leader ruled the roost on that street. Her word was law—no one dared oppose her. She owned a four-storey house a couple of dwellings away, on the opposite side from our residence. If we ever happened to cross her path when she was sitting in the front yard of our house, we had to touch her feet on our way out.

We followed her rules; she carried out her decision to evict us from the street. Nani was a great help in this difficult situation. While she sent other kothis to Shivaji Nagar, she allowed me to stay with Priya and Prateeksha, who both belonged to the Punekar parivar—a different parivar from my own.

Priya and Prateeksha managed to rent a house belonging to an 'autovala' of the Lonavala autorickshaw stand. It was brave of the owner to show us confidence in a locality where tirunangais were not welcome tenants.

Priya and Prateeksha funded the rental advance and the purchase of vessels, utensils and other essentials. For my contribution, I paid them an additional amount every month, along with my share of the rent. The house was located in an area of Lonavala that was neither urban nor rural. Our house, which was one half of a twin house, offered a view of the hills and dunes. It was a beautiful, little house: simple and neat. It had a hall spacious enough for the three of us, and a kitchen. We were dropped at the railway station every morning in the landlord's autorickshaw.

We were soon joined by a tirunangai answering to the improbable name of Titanic. She had recently arrived at Priya's nani's house.

Titanic was a good cook. Priya wasn't too bad in the culinary arts either. As for Prateeksha and I...well, let's say we were good at eating.

Titanic cooked two meals every morning. We'd eat breakfast before leaving home and carry a packed lunch. Before her arrival, we generally ate at the railway station. Misal Pav—a spicy mixture of dal and chana, eaten with pav bread—was a speciality available at Khandala, Karjat and Lonavala. I didn't like it at first, but began to relish it over time—especially Khandala's.

We changed our routes to suit our move to Lonavala. As the dol had grown bigger, we also needed a bigger field for our exploits. The fun-and-games factor was still on the rise in our group. As the railway workers and officials were now our friends, we kept our lunch boxes in their dining rooms for the morning. They were so friendly that they kept them safe for us until we went there to eat.

We must have been the only train-begging tirunangais who actually took packed lunches with them, like regular office-going commuters. Our leisurely lunches at the canteen along with railway employees, followed by our journeys with them, must surely have made onlookers wonder. We were a privileged lot, weren't we?

Between lunch and the next train at 4.00, we generally sat on a bench outside the booking counter, playing games in the shade of nearby trees. We would frequently pretend to be a family, as mothers-in-law and daughters-in-law, mothers and daughters, and so on. We had mock fights, and chased one another around like schoolgirls.

We wanted to live like other women; we wanted to be home-makers. Nature decreed a neutral existence. It was a sad burden we had to bear. These games helped reduce that burden a bit.

We never tired of our games. Sometimes, Priya mimicked scenes from English movies dubbed into Telugu for our amusement. She also performed dances from old Telugu films. In the evenings, we switched on the cassette recorder and entertained ourselves. Priya and I did some group dances from films. Prateeksha was a hopeless dancer, and her awkward attempts always drew a laugh from all of us. Titanic's efforts were equally diverting. With her swarthy complexion, plump figure, and a face that was a comedienne's delight, she brought the roof down every time she danced to a love song, replete with all the passionate gesticulations you see on screen. Even the young girls and boys wandering about the station joined us in enjoying a laugh at Titanic's expense, all in good fun.

Occasionally we wore jeans and T-shirts, relieving ourselves of formal saris in favour of more casual attire. Our Lonavala days will always stay with me. I still miss Prateeksha, Priya, Titanic and the wonderful times we had together. Isn't friendship the most beautiful gift of life?

Chatla

For the first fifteen days of my begging career, my extreme diffidence made it difficult for me to put my hand out in supplication—especially for alms. Shame, fear, ego, my education, memories of awards and rewards and God knows what else made me pull back every time I tried.

But soon enough I got over all that and managed to shed my feelings of guilt about begging. I started clapping and demanding alms like the average tirunangai.

True, I was a graduate—an MA in linguistics, in fact—but did that mean there were government jobs waiting for me, a transgender person? And while there might be sympathizers in the private sector, how many would actively support tirunangais? If I wanted to strike the path of a self-employed entrepreneur, how many people would be ready to give me business, or even finance my venture? There is absolutely no social security for transgenders in this country. Who will step forward to help us, when the government itself is unprepared to extend any kind of basic recognition—it does not issue us a voter ID or even a ration card!

The realization hit me hard that any revolution in trends of gender discrimination—including discrimination against transgenders—was merely lip service, and that begging was my only practical source of income. I made up my mind immediately—I could not blame anyone for the state of affairs.

Insults heaped on me and all my shattered hopes repeatedly reinforced the fact that I was not considered a member of this society. The object of everyone's ridicule for so long, I came to regard all of society as something ridiculous—I came to believe that the world was full of mad men, within which I had to live with my body, my pain, my sorrows.

People generally feel they are living in a good world—a world free from corruption, violence, betrayal, treachery, obscenity and greed. But how many slings and arrows of outrageous fortune has this world directed at me! These missiles have battered my heart to numbness. When I go out and beg—on the street, in trains, at shops—I consider it my revenge, my claim of compensation from each and every member of the prevailing society.

No longer guilty or humiliated, I set out on my shop-begging campaign with happiness.

I approached my 'customers' in different ways—cajoling, pleading, teasing. Appealing to their better nature, I blessed them, addressing them as brother, uncle, sister, so on and so forth. 'You earn so much in a day, why can't you spare some of it happily for a transgender?' 'Give with love, happily. Think of your family, your children, and give with a generous heart.' 'You are such a big shot, but so miserly. Can't you do better than a rupee?' Cycling through every possible variation, I made an art form of begging.

Inside, I simmered with rage against a formless, nameless society. Begging in stores was no joke: bazaar begging meant walking miles and miles everyday, stopping at shop after shop. Nobody gave you a red carpet welcome; the security staff at big shops refused to let you in, so you had to shout at them and make a racket; you had to clap till your hands stung even when you had long stopped clapping: only then did they give you any alms—reluctantly, to be rid of a nuisance, not out of any sympathy.

Train begging was no different: you walked all day long; you were constantly in moving trains; you had to change your money before the next train and run from one platform to another; you needed the mental maturity to tackle poisonous barbs, even if your feelings were dead.

Once a Tamil woman in a train asked me, 'Aren't you ashamed to beg? Aren't you able-bodied?'

I lost my cool. Normally, we never beg from women other than college students or mothers with infants—women do not even have the right to give alms in this wretched male- dominated society. Sometimes, women travelling with their families look at us with some pity, and we try to get them to influence their husbands to give us money. Young mothers are a sure bet, as they would like their babies to be blessed.

I was not seeking alms from that woman that day, but had only approached the man next to her. She addressed those remarks to me when I started to move away towards the next seat.

My retort was angry: 'Do you want me to die? Can't you see I am begging shamelessly? What do you lose by giving me five rupees? Will you build a fortress with the money you save? Instead of giving me advice, why don't you get me a job in your husband's company?'

She didn't back off. 'Why should I get you a job?' she asked. 'D'you think I have nothing else to do?'

'Hey, why don't you attend to whatever else you have to do then? Why do you have to argue with a beggar? Can't give five paise, but want to travel in a reserved compartment!'

Normally courteous, I could, on occasion, show my temper too!

Sometimes, passengers pretend to be asleep or absorbed in a book, no matter how much noise you make. I used to get so irritated on such occasions. Though I normally walked away quietly, there were times when I wanted to spit in their faces and ask them uncomfortable questions.

Most of my bad experiences in Pune were at the hands of Tamils. One such instance was on the Nagerkoil train. It wasn't very crowded that day; I didn't collect even five rupees in the first compartment. A terrifying experience was waiting around the corner for me, as I entered the second compartment. A foursome was sitting there: three of the men were tall and well built; the fourth one seemed to be a kindly person. I avoided the toughies and approached the softie. He gave me two rupees. 'Can't you make it five, Tamil sir?' I said. Hardly had I spoken when a hard slap landed on my cheek. It was delivered by the buffalo sitting in the opposite seat. 'Hasn't he given you two rupees? How dare you ask for more?'

I reacted instantly. 'Slipper you! How dare you hit me, you dog?' I said.

All hell broke loose—all four converged on me and attacked me fiercely. I somehow escaped after much struggle and moved away.

My hands and legs were trembling; tears were coursing down my cheeks. I was full of self-pity. Wasn't I going through all this trauma for money? I looked at the two-rupee coin. It was suddenly a huge burden.

I toyed with the idea of flinging the coin out of the door, but changed my mind. I strode purposefully back towards the compartment and stood amidst the same four passengers. I bit the coin, circled my head with it, muttered some curses directed against them, and threw the coin out of the train.

It was a firm belief among tirunangais that if you did what I did, cursing your antagonist, he would surely experience financial troubles. Many among the general public, too, believed in this superstition.

Now four or five people surrounded me again: one of them held my arms and intertwined them between the stairs of the ladder to the upper berth; another pulled my hair; a third thug whipped me with the buckled end of his belt, hitting my face. His wild swing found my cheekbone and I started bleeding. It hurt like hell, but I didn't weep. I shouted angrily at them, 'Get lost, you sissies! You impotent dogs, can't you do better than show your bravado to a woman like me? Why don't you take on men your size and display your heroism? Otherwise wear a sari and come and strut before me.'

I was screaming at the top of my voice, unable to cope with the pain, drawing a whole compartment of spectators to our cubicle. None of the onlookers made any attempt to rescue me or push my aggressors back. They were more interested in watching the fun.

They continued to beat me and I continued to scream. When the train stopped at Pimpri, someone shouted, 'Push the creature out!'

Finally, they pushed me out at the next stop; however, still scared I would get back in, they were all set to drive me away.

Once the train started, I ran and got into the next compartment—it was a general compartment. I cursed my assailants with all the swearwords in my vocabulary.

My nose was bleeding, my face was all swollen, my whole body ached; I looked—to myself—like some kind of monster.

I found a human being in the compartment—a fifty-year old woman. 'Poor child, how they've hammered you!' she said, comforting me. 'Please wipe your nose.' I continued to weep, feeling deeply sorry for my plight. The pain, disgrace, and helplessness of it all hurt me profoundly.

You can bear most of the troubles of life, but to feel orphaned is to feel a huge loss—self-pity is a strong drug, a venom: what I was undergoing was such thorough misery.

Violent incidents took place predominantly when I was begging alone. It was for this reason I teamed up with Priya and Prateeksha. There were advantages to begging in a group of three or four. For one thing, we could support one another in situations like those on the train. The public are also wary of us in a group. On top of all that was Priya's hot temper, which was matched only by her playfulness.

Once, when she was begging in the bazaar alone, a man made to attack her. She took a brick in hand and stood there defying him as if she were the Hindu goddess Bhadrakali, the destroyer of evil. 'Come on, I'm ready for you. Come, I am ready to risk my life,' she said, and most unexpectedly hit herself on the head with the brick. When she started bleeding profusely, her would-be assailant ran away.

So I decided it was wise to join a dol. Once, a military man and his friend came into the compartment: both were massively built. Even though we did not approach them for alms, the army man tried to drive us out. 'Get lost,' he kept saying.

'Look at this great man threatening us! Mind your business,' Priya said to him.

I added my two bits' worth. 'We see thousands of men like you on the train,' I said. 'Don't try to show off. Did we ask you for money? Don't try to throw your weight around.'

He looked so frightening, we decided to make a quiet exit. 'Look at the way these beggar dogs talk,' the military man waved us off after raising his hand to beat us. But he did not spare Priya, who let us go first and followed after—he hit her.

That was the signal for all of us to retaliate. We were so angry that Priya, Prateeksha and I stood in front of him with all the courage we could muster. 'How dare you strike a female?' Priya screamed at him. 'Who cares if you are a soldier? Come with us to the Pune police station. We'll hold a parade for you there. All the transgenders will be waiting for you. We won't let you cross Pune. Just wait and see.' She turned to me and said, 'Call Nani now.'

I called Nani on my mobile phone and pretended to mobilize the whole community to gather at Pune station. We managed to put on a great act. The men certainly had not expected such an outcry from us, and were terrified at the prospect of an army of tirunangais greeting them in Pune.

Some onlookers advised the men to settle the issue by giving us some money. 'Why do you want to antagonize these people? Just give them some ten rupees and get rid of them.'

Having put the fear of God in the army man, we left him alone and moved on to the next compartment. We had frightened him so much that we ran the risk of his going to the police for protection.

Our gift of gab had saved us. We got off the train even before it reached the station—jumping off as it waited outside and running away out of sight past the tracks.

There was never any shortage of such perils and humiliations. Nonetheless, I was obsessively collecting and saving money throughout. I desperately needed money—not to buy fancy stuff but to redeem my identity, to fulfil my dream, to achieve what I set out for in Pune: nirvana.

Nirvana was an operation—the operation that would slash and remove the sin of my birth as a male. I needed to save for it, though. The sooner I collected the money, the sooner I'd have nirvana.

My survival after the surgery was a question mark: I was told I had a fifty-fifty chance. That was no big deal—I had to die some day. Sure enough about wanting to discard my male identity, I was willing to die in the process.

In countries where sex change operations are legal, many tests are performed on the person undergoing the procedure—medical, investigative, environmental and RLT (real life testing). The tests are done over a period of six to eighteen months, and ultimately a psychiatrist and gynaecologist have to recommend sex reassignment surgery (SRS). The operation is extremely expensive, and the recovery takes at least three months. The pain is unimaginable.

SRS can incorporate facial feminization, speech therapy, breast augmentation and the insertion of a plastic vagina. You can acquire the sweet voice of a normal woman. Your new name and sex change are duly marked in all the identity documents you will ever need, including your degree certificates, if you should have any. Thus, one is enabled to seek proper employment or return to an earlier job.

The story is different in India. What happens here is no SRS. What we undergo here is merely castration under local anaesthesia—and that too without government approval. An illegal procedure, its fruits include a lack of social approval, such as denial of jobs and opportunities for higher education. Transgenders in India have no option but to resort to begging or prostitution.

Why then should we undergo this illegal operation? One would be right to ask such a question. The only answer is that a person of my kind never feels male. Our male identity is an unfortunate accident. We are—we want to be—women. We feel like women.

If you are a man, would you like to wear women's clothes and go to work? If you are a woman, would you like hirsute facial growth?

That is the essence of our problem—my problem. We are women at heart desperately seeking to delete or erase our male identity. That is why we crave the surgical procedure that will give us the bodily likeness of that female identity.

Unfortunately, these operations are carried out in primitive, unsafe, unhygienic conditions in India. A kothi undergoing castration is not administered any tests. No questions are asked either. The kothi only learns the fee payable—ranging from three to ten thousand rupees, depending on the place where it is done.

The only test done is to determine if the kothi is HIV positive, which test is performed with a view to collecting extra fees from the kothi, not for any medical purpose.

The hospital where my operation took place was low on hygiene. I was not even given a proper bed—just a steel cot with a newspaper spread on it. The surgeon gave me no guarantees, no counselling. The only pre-operation preparation was anaesthesia—that too a local injection. They castrate you while you are watching, suture in the next few minutes, clean you with cotton and pack you off to recover. 'Next!' they call out after.

The post-operative pain is indescribable. You want to die—and people often do. The operation is no different from a procedure performed at the butcher's shop.

Afterward, you are left with a hole to pass urine through—a task that remains painful and messy until the wound heals. You can't move your legs for a few days, so you cry and scream all day long from your bed, to no avail.

Elder tirunangais sit with you to comfort you. The hospital discharges you at the earliest opportunity, the moment you start to feel a little better. Within three or four days, you are back at home.

My operation was made worse by the poor effectiveness of the anaesthetic. They had to give me a second shot, as the first did not work—and even then I felt pain during the operation. How could I expect better treatment at that hospital? I didn't even know its name—it had no sign board.

Remember how Satya, Nagarani and I had the operation at the same time. Of the three of us, Satya bore the pain best. Naturally the toughest among us, she was up and about within two days, while I was still struggling three days after the surgery.

They dumped me on a bare cot immediately after the operation. The pain was unbearable and kept getting worse. I screamed and shouted non-stop. I begged the nurse to give me an injection to kill the pain while she was negotiating a higher tip with Sugandhi Ayah.

The second day after the operation was a little better. Satya was already walking around. I took another day to start hobbling, after which the hospital discharged me immediately. No medicines were prescribed; no regimen was recommended; no after-effects or side effects were explained. It was up to me to manage my recovery on my own.

Sugandhi Ayah took us gingerly by autorickshaw to the Cuddapah railway station. The way we limped, with our legs spread wide, drew laughs all around. I bore all the taunts stoically believing in the promise of impending freedom.

We got into an unreserved compartment in the train and reached Chennai. We didn't even have seats! The journey was a forgettable struggle.

From the station we went to Vyasarpadi, to Neelamma's residence. A good sort, if irritable, she was paid to look after us for the next forty days. We didn't mind her irritability, though. Such was her nature and she took care of us well.

She fed us regularly for those forty days and helped us overcome the pain. We underwent the ritual of standing in the bathroom while hot water was splashed on our wounds—a home remedy to prevent infection. Neelamma would help me clean up, change the dressing and so on.

By the time the pain subsided, the wound had healed substantially. The moment I had waited for all my life had arrived: I was a woman now, no longer a man. What more could I want?

Haldi mehndi followed—a ritual announcement to the transgender community that I was now one of them—at a kalyana mandapam at Vyasarpadi. Many of Chennai's tirunangais attended the function, which began in the evening and went on till well after midnight.

I was made to wear a pavadai and sit down, while tirunangais queued up to apply marudani—the green leaf paste that turns red on drying—to my plans. They also smeared turmeric paste on my face, arms and feet. After affixing a huge bindi on my forehead, they put some sugar on my tongue. Finally, they waved currency notes—ten, twenty, fifty rupees—around my head to ward off evil influences.

All the tirunangais then started to sing and dance and make merry. Recorded music blared while the merriment continued. All through the party, the 'drishti' ritual—waving currency notes and actually throwing them on the floor—continued around me.

It was past two o'clock when I went to have a ritual bath. After that, I was made to wear a green sari, a green blouse, green bangles and other green ornaments. I was given a jug of milk to announce the climax of the evening's entertainment.

They took me to the seashore, milk jug in hand. I had to pour the milk into the sea, stand facing it, and reveal my healed private parts to the expanse of the ocean. This was the moment of completion of my nirvana—the moment of announcing my identity to nature.

The next step was to repeat the procedure in front of a black dog. Finally, I had to do it once more before a green tree.

This ritual is known as chatla. It is a time-honoured ceremony among tirunangais.

Satya and I completed the ceremony successfully and prepared to go back to Pune.

Henceforth I would be a tirunangai—complete. This alone was my identity.

Sales experience

My experience was akin to spring cleaning—like cleaning an old house, removing the cobwebs and dust, swabbing the floors and whitewashing the walls. My woman's body no longer had a male protuberance. This sense of freedom was at the fore of my awareness as I returned to Pune from nirvana, forty days of recuperation, and the ritual initiation into womanhood.

I didn't go out to beg at shops the first two days, and Nani didn't force me to. I spent that time talking to everyone and sharing my recent experiences. Meanwhile, a new yearning began to make its presence felt inside me: the urge to go to Tiruchi and meet my family—Radha, Manju, Chithi, Appa, Prabha, all of them. If the long interval since the last time I saw all of them was one motivating factor, the other was guilt at not visiting them from Chennai when I was camping there.

I was sure Nani would turn my request down, give me a lecture and make sarcastic remarks; and yet, to my surprise, she not only acquiesced, but actually gave me money for expenses. That was really generous of her, as she had incurred substantial expenses because of me these past few months, over and above the loss of earnings during my leave of absence.

With the money that Nani gave me, I bought saris for Radha, Manju and Chithi, a fashionable pair of churidars for Prabha, a scent bottle for Appa, and set off on my journey home.

From Tiruchi I went straight to Radha's house. Some of my acquaintances on the street directed covert glances at me and walked away without uttering even a greeting. My appearance and clothes must have caused them a palpitation or two. I ignored them and knocked on Radha's door unannounced.

Even though Akka had at least somewhat accepted my new identity, I burst into tears as soon as I saw her—the tears just came. She immediately informed everyone, and Appa, Chithi, and Manju arrived from Uyyakkondan Tirumalai to meet me. Manju, Mama and their children, Balaji and Pappathi, also came. Radha's and Manju's children did not recognize me.

All of them must have lost hope of ever meeting me again. My reassurances of a bright future notwithstanding, they surely knew the difficulties of the path of a tirunangai, and expected me to stay away from home, ashamed of myself. When I actually belied their fears and came home after a long gap, they were all overcome by emotion. Manju, in particular, was speechless on seeing me. Radha and Chithi recovered enough to have some conversation with me—I had been in touch with them over the phone from Pune—as they had had time enough to accept the situation to some extent.

All three of them kept asking me to stay back. Appa was stiff as always, but his pleasure at having me back was visible—it showed on his face.

I stayed for two days, generally eating and sleeping and chatting with everyone. The moment I felt it was time to go, I took off. Radha borrowed money from a friend and gave me 3,500 rupees, which I accepted after much protest.

Within a month of my return from Tiruchi to Pune, Priya went to Chennai on a month-long vacation. As her family had accepted her gender change, she went home annually for a month.

Her mother, brother and married elder sister treated her with much love, and her father was no more. Back in Pune, she sent home money every month.

Our dol was short of members, both in the absence of Priya and because of Titanic, who had gone away for her nirvana. Prateeksha and I did the shop rounds by ourselves.

I was less motivated to beg in shops now than I had been before. Maybe the lack of the obsessive desire to save up for nirvana was the difference. Now that I had achieved my goal, the intensity was missing. The knowledge that I could live as I pleased was uppermost in my thoughts. My income started sliding.

'Hey new girl! Does the baby find it difficult to ask for alms after nirvana?' Nani asked me. 'Unless you earn now, how will you survive at my age? Don't you want to live in some dignity and contribute to the household as well. No jobs are waiting out there—your degrees will get you nowhere. You'd better do the sensible thing and concentrate on begging.'

She was absolutely right. How could I find employment in a country which did not recognize people like us, where there was no social concern for us, no legal status, where even family support was non-existent? Leave alone old age—even the present was precarious. What would I do were I to fall ill?

I had to save for the future to survive in a world ruled by material considerations. Poor Vasanti Ayah was still forced to beg on trains because she did not save in her youth, despite her substantial earnings.

One day, Vasanti Ayah told us the story of four tirunangais who lived opposite our house. They went away to Surat on learning that there was far less competition from other tirunangais there. They were doing very well for themselves on the train beat.

'Shall we go there, too?' I asked Prateeksha, thinking the change of scene and different culture might do us good.

We took Vasanti Ayah with us and went to Surat, reaching there by trial and error, hopping from train to train and begging along the way. Spreading newspapers on the floor, we slept on the steps leading from the tracks to the platform. It was very cold at night, and we also had to fend off competition from an old man who staked a claim to the sleeping spot we chose. By the time we hit the sack, it was ten o'clock. We had been on our feet begging till eight.

Working the Surat railway station was less profitable than we had anticipated. We cut short our proposed stay of a week to three days, and were on the verge of going back, when Prateeksha had an idea. She had heard that quality textiles were available at competitive prices, and after hurried consultations we arrived at a new business proposal—to buy saris at Surat and sell them on the train. We returned to Pune excited, dreaming about our new business; but our excitement was short-lived, as we soon found that we did not have sufficient money to invest to achieve any kind of economy of scale.

We thought of alternative businesses to engage in rather than continuing to ask for alms. After some intensive brainstorming, we decided we would sell simple articles on the train instead. I had a good friend, Abu, who was a canteen manager on the Karjat train, on the Mumbai-Sholapur route. A married man, he first befriended me because he was impressed by my gentle, courteous behaviour even whilst seeking alms. Once he knew that I had a postgraduate degree, he started treating me with respect. He introduced me to many first class passengers, trying to elicit their sympathy by highlighting the fact that I was begging despite my qualifications, all in the hope that one of them would help me find a job.

Abu often encouraged me to start a small business selling tea and biscuits on the train rather than begging. He even promised to help me in the business.

Prateeksha and I decided to plunge into action. With great hesitation, we approached Nani for permission. Nani had a very good opinion of me—I was the only one who was never physically punished by her. Even Satya received the occasional slap. In fact, Nani never even raised her voice at me. She liked the fact that I had no vices—no tobacco, supari or betel chewing habit—and had even offered to put me in college if I wanted to study further.

Nani was surprised that I wanted to start a business now, after turning down her offer to send me to college. At the same time, she was impressed by my determination to alter our livelihood. She raised no objections, but gave us her blessings only after cautioning us against the risks.

One of Prateeksha's friends, Kumar, ran away from home when he was ten years old. Married at sixteen, a father of two kids at twenty-seven, he sold a variety of small articles on trains. His stock of goods ranged from keychains to pouches for mobile phones. He not only encouraged us in our new venture, but taught us where to buy goods at the best wholesale prices and how to promote our products in the train, taking two full days off his own business to take us round to suppliers. With assurances that our lives would be transformed by the new venture, he sent us off on our first day with his best wishes.

What a superb experience that was! We set out with great expectations and our hearts full of happiness. The two of us went different ways in the same train, dividing the products between us. We tried every trick known to plug our products—stressing both their superior quality and their competitive pricing, for instance.

Hour after hour we roamed the compartments, without being able to sell anything. From bogey to bogey we advertised our wares, loud and clear, but all we got in return were aching feet and sore throats.

It was tough. People were not interested in buying anything from us—even those who used to give us alms would turn the other way when we passed them with our products and pitches. The gentlemen who exhorted us to work hard for a living whenever we begged were suddenly oddly absent.

We were dog tired when we returned home after shouting ourselves hoarse all day long. Neither of us had ever expected our first venture to end in such complete failure.

'We don't know how to sell,' I consoled myself. 'We'll learn as we go along. Business will pick up soon.' Prateeksha was hardly in any frame of mind to talk.

Kumar was taken by surprise as well, and accompanied us the next day. As we went ahead with our sales cries, he followed, observing our tactics. He was quite satisfied that we were doing all the right things.

Even other vendors on the train, who should have viewed us as competition, encouraged us and wished us well. None of the daily commuters came forward with even a two-rupee purchase to kickstart our venture. Puzzlingly, the travelling ticket examiners, who looked the other way when we begged, were now creating trouble for us.

The second day was equally a washout. Completely dejected, we sat down at Shivaji station, where Kumar joined us. He tried to cheer us up. 'Don't lose heart after just two days of effort,' he advised us. Buying all our stock himself by paying a proper price for them, he suggested that we concentrate on the local trains, selling ten-rupee torches. We tried out his suggestion.

Though we managed to increase sales with flashlights and keychains on the local trains—which carried many more Tamil passengers—than on the Nagerkoil and Coimbatore trains, the take was not substantially better. Unlike the long distance trains, the local trains were very frequent, and we had to get on and off rapidly. We did our best, not minding the severe hard work, but the returns were not good enough. The problem was obviously our gender, not the goods we sold. We couldn't understand the prejudice. What did it matter who sold the goods, so long as the goods were of acceptable quality and price?

I had been dreaming of starting small and building big. In my dreams, we were going to own a shop in the near future. For someone who loved to daydream, it was hard to see these crash so rudely to the floor. Prateeksha and I received a proper dressing down from Nani.

I was consumed by the desire to lead a dignified life, to put an end to begging on trains or in marketplaces, but was forced by circumstances to go back to alms. On an auspicious day, we returned to the old routine.

Now a number of rozwalas, including some who had never spoken to us before, started commiserating with us, asking us why we were back on our old beat and what had happened to our attempted business. Nothing came of it all except their sympathies, elicited by our sorrowful descriptions.

I was deeply upset—my carefree, happy life had been turned upside down. To further my despondancy, some incidents occurred that wounded me deeper. One such was an encounter with Mr Ramanujam—an actor and theatre personality I hugely respected, whom I knew personally, and had even visited at home—who was seated one day in a compartment of the Hyderabad train.

Mr Ramanujam is a genius. Responsible for the creation of the Tamil University, he was Mu Ra's role model. He had dedicated his whole life to theatre. Not wanting to stand before him as a beggar, I did not even hesitate for a moment, but flew from his presence in a flash.

How low had my life sunk! I felt miserable, and stopped begging for the day. In the evening, I phoned 'Othigai' Vijay and Murugabhupati, and cried over the phone as I told them what had happened.

'Please get me a job there, anna,' I pleaded. 'Please try. I can't stay here. Let me come back.'

Murugabhupati promised to help. It was comforting to hear him say so, but I was restless. Once I set my mind on something, I had to accomplish it, whatever it took to do it. At the same time, all the fortunes of the world are unable to make me do something I don't care to do. Begging I took to willingly, with concerted effort, and now the decision to quit was taking firm root in me. I instantly decided to give it up forever.

My decision to seek employment dampened my enthusiasm for begging expeditions at shops. I tended to be half-hearted in my daily forays, and my earnings duly plummeted. Prateeksha understood my predicament. She longed for me to find a job to put an end to my misery. My only hope lay in Murugabhupati's assurance, so I decided to leave Pune, come what might.

Days and months passed with no job in sight. My hopes began to dwindle. I followed up on a weekly basis with Othigai Viji and Murugabhupati.

'You come here first. Only then can we start looking for a job for you. We can't help you long distance,' Viji told me once. Fair enough! I decided to try my luck at Madurai. That would be my last ditch effort. It would be great to find a job, and I could always come back to Nani if I didn't succeed.

How could I convince Nani and receive her permission? Running away from Lonavala without informing anyone was an option, but that would land Prateeksha in trouble. I didn't want to leave my dear friend in such a difficult fix.

Unable to even pack my suitcase without Nani's knowledge, unsure she would allow me to go, I was on the horns of a dilemma.

I tried to find a solution that would not harm anyone.

Back to struggle

Monsoon. Torrential rains lashed the state of Maharashtra. Trains were cancelled; rail tracks were damaged; offices, schools and colleges were frequently closed; shopping complexes were deserted. From whom could I beg in the heavy rain?

I decided to leave Lonavala on this pretext, without hurting Prateeksha's interests. I would sell my move to Nani on professional grounds, and play it by ear thereafter.

'Nani, let me go to Vaidawadi,' I said.

'You don't want to go on the train?' Nani asked innocently.

I told her the rains had affected business and offered to stay in Vaidawadi for a while, saying I would return to Lonavala after the rainy season to work on the trains again.

Nani agreed, and I booked my train tickets at Lonavala. I was to stay at one of Nani's two houses at Vaidawadi—nice, simple houses, where families lived. Malar—Parimala Ammal's chela—lived there. Conveniently for me, however, she had gone to visit her home town.

The move was not entirely convenient, though, for Nani did not send me alone. I was left responsible not only for the Vaidawadi household until Malar's return, but also for Subbu and Sheba, both younger than me.

Subbu was a sweet person. Dark complexioned and

mischief-eyed, she wore a bandana on her head, as her hair hadn't grown fully yet. She was talkative, but a good friend. When I reached Vaidawadi with my two sisters, my only thought was to go back home and take up a job. I wanted to be independent.

I would need money for that ticket, and I had an obligation to beg along with my sisters, so we went to the shops for ten days. The rains intensified and areas around Lonavala were badly hit. Radha was getting worried about me. I promised her I would be home soon and made my train reservations.

Tragedy struck on the day I planned to leave. The rains reached unprecedented levels and Mumbai was badly affected. Many parts of the city were flooded, people were stranded and many lives were lost. I watched the floods of July 2005— remembered all over India as a major disaster in Mumbai and many parts of Maharashtra—from a safe enough distance.

All road traffic came to a standstill and all trains were cancelled. After four or five days, I cancelled my earlier reservation and booked a fresh ticket.

The day I left, I had arranged for an autorickshaw to pick me up at midnight. Travelling late at night was safer than travelling by day—I didn't want to be seen by anyone who could report my departure with bag and baggage to Nani. I had to protect Subbu and Sheba by leaving without their knowledge. They would come to no harm, as they were young.

I kept wide awake as my sisters slept. When the autorickshaw came at midnight, I slipped out quietly with my luggage and some money I had saved from ten days of begging. The train, which was due at 1.00 a.m., was delayed. Announcements were made intermittently, but the train finally came at 4.00 a.m. Every moment of waiting was scary, for I didn't want to be spotted by anyone. What if someone at home woke up and started looking for me?

When a tirunangai went missing, a search party invariably landed at the railway station. If caught, you really had to face the music. The enquiry that followed was quite a harrowing experience. People who were loving all along could turn quite cruel; and if Nani saw my attempt to leave as an act of betrayal, it would spell disaster for me.

I huddled like a thief at the station where until the day before I had reigned as a queen. In addition to the fear of discovery, I was also scared of men trying to molest me. I have been firm in my resolve to never be a sex worker, and have maintained my principles; even my begging had its basis in wanting enough money to undergo SRS. Now I was determined to leave that part of my life behind and head for a career.

The train I took was bound for Coimbatore. Chances of detection by Nani's people were lower on this train than on a Chennai bound train. Her representatives would surely be waiting for me at Chennai Central. After boarding, I covered myself from head to toe and slept.

I spent the day on the train in introspection, remembering my past, dreaming of my future, worrying about what lay ahead. I got off the train at Erode station, happy to be back in Tamil Nadu, but unsure where to go or what to do next. I could go home, but that had its problems—they would surely be happy to have me there forever; but as a man, not as a woman. If they insisted I change my identity again, I would be unable to obey them.

All my problems were of my own making, but I cannot accept responsibility for the troubles my wants and desires created for others. I liked Pune, where I could live as a woman, but to live there I would have to beg or be a sex worker. And so I left.

I embarked on a train bound for Karur—my friends had promised to help me find a job in Tamil Nadu. Until I found employment, I knew I had to depend on someone for my living expenses, but it was essential that dependence did not lead to any compromises. I was still lost in deep thought about my future when the train reached Karur station around 8.30 p.m. This was where Manju lived.

It had been years since I last came to Karur. Manju's house was a short walk from the station, and I debated visiting her, deciding finally against it because many people on the platform were already staring at me in my jeans and T-shirt. What would I have in common with Manju's uncle, aunt, brother-in-law and other members of their family? They would probably tease Manju about me after I left. No, I would not go. I was determined to protect my sister from ridicule.

My next stop was certainly Tiruchi. Not Appa's house, but Radha's was my only destination there. She never made a fuss whenever I knocked at her door late at night, especially during my rehearsals for *The 18th Battle*. So Radha's house it was! I went there straight from the station.

She welcomed me warmly when I reached. 'Ennada, how come you have arrived with bag and baggage!' The 'da' in 'ennada' (enna means what) is a familiar form of address meant for a male, and I reacted immediately.

'Haven't I told you I don't like your calling me "da"? My name is Vidya, by the way.'

Radha laughed and invited me in.

I told her I was going to stay there for some time and do some serious job hunting. 'Can I stay here until I find a job?' I asked. She raised no objections to my plans.

The first thing I did was call Murugabhupati and Selvam. They were both actively on the job of looking for one for me.

I decided to make a visit to Thanjavur. Scared of being spotted by old acquaintances, I took the ten o'clock train, which was not usually crowded. After changing to a bus, with old memories accompanying me all the way, I reached the university. At the drama department, I stood before Professor Mu Ramaswami, who did not show any great surprise on seeing me in a female form. He looked worried, though.

He was disappointed I did not complete my PhD before leaving for Pune. When I asked if I could do it then, he promised to speak to the vice chancellor and try to register me as a candidate.

I was tempted to register as a PhD candidate with the help and guidance of Mu Ra, but it would pose problems. For one, I didn't have the wherewithal to support myself for the four years or so it would take.

'I'll think about it, sir,' I told him. 'Please help me find a safe place to stay and a job in the meantime.' Over the next few days I visited the university regularly, seeing Viji in between.

I also met my old friends at the university at every possible occasion. They were very good to me, careful not to wound my feelings. They did not ask me embarrassing questions. My fears had been unfounded.

All of them wanted to know what I was going to do next. They all wished me luck when I told them about my PhD plans.

My classmates Ramalakshmi and Subhasri treated me like a girl, making me feel at home. They used the intimate form of address among girls, 'dee', freely with me. 'Vidya, this pair of jeans looks good on you,' one of them said. Another advised me on the size of bindi I should affix on my forehead. A third recommended the use of turmeric for a better complexion. I spent a happy day in the company of girls.

I met Nehru and spoke about my confusion to him, requesting that he look for a sponsor to help me study. Another friend I called on was the director of *The 18th Battle*, Muthuvel Azhagan. He was very upset with what I had done to myself, and chided me for not approaching him for help instead of undergoing sex change. 'I know the pain and suffering you must have undergone,' he said. He had visited tirunangais at the Koovagam congress, and was familiar with transgenders, but simply could not accept me as Vidya. 'Think of me as your father,' he said. 'Don't hesitate to ask for help.' I reiterated my request for help in securing employment.

The whole team of my well-wishers were on a job hunt for me—Nehru, Mu Ra, Murugabhupati, Selvam, Viji, all of them—but time seemed to be running out. And then I suffered a setback to my health—a severe attack of stomach ache. The pain worsened all the time, eventually getting so bad that my uncle took me to a hospital on the cantonment road. The hospital staff were quite bemused by my appearance, wearing a kurta and bermuda shorts, earrings, nose ring and all. They prescribed me medication after some routine tests and discharged me. When I went home, the pain just refused to go away and, in fact, continued to worsen. We returned to the hospital and I was admitted as an in-patient this time. They gave me drips and kept me under observation, as the senior doctor was not available at night.

The next morning Radha came to see me. A scan revealed acute appendicitis. Immediate surgery was indicated. I was so scared of surgery—and it would cost quite a bomb. My family thought of shifting me to the government hospital, but decided against it. They didn't want to expose me to the unhygienic conditions there.

Eventually I agreed to the operation, overcoming fears caused by my earlier experience. When the inevitable question came— 'Have you ever undergone any surgery before?'—I shocked the nurse with my reply. Lest complications result, I explained the whole story to her in detail.

Before the operation I had to undergo a million tests. How

on earth did I survive all those? My operation was performed
in a spacious theatre, on a comfortable bed—luxuries I hadn't
known before. Many people were around me, but I couldn't open
my eyes or sense who they were. Even though I was told the
operation was successful, the pain was intense, and I screamed in
agony. Radha said, 'How did you go through the earlier operation
if you find this one so difficult to bear, da?' I once again showed
irritation at her calling me 'da'.

Nehru did not visit me at the hospital, but his wife did.
Many members of my family and friends visited me.

I received plenty of advice, which I suffered along with
the pain for four days. My case became famous in the nursing
home, and I made friends with all the nurses. The last couple
of days chatting with the nurses and sending messages on my
mobile phone to my friends were enjoyable, and in a week's
time I was discharged.

One important outcome of the ordeal was the inclusion in the
discharge certificate of the observation: 'Male to female operation
done in Pune.' This was the first written documentation of the
sex change I had undergone.

I went to Radha's house after the operation, full of guilt at
causing great expenditure to her and the family. Mama would
never resent playing host to me, even for extended periods,
though he hardly approved of my going around in kurta-skirt,
earrings, nose stud and so on.

My health improved. During the day I wore women's clothes
and went to Thanjavur, and at night I wore a kurta. Most of
the time I felt like a worm—I stayed aloof from all, cowering
in a corner, unable to sleep at night, going crazy with anxiety.
When would I find a job?

Irritated with my appearance, Mama castigated me out of
sheer frustration: 'When you can go to your father's home dressed

like a man, taking off all your jewellery, why do you act like a woman here? Aren't we human, too? Aren't there people around us? How many questions I have to answer about you! What insults, what humiliation! Take off that nose stud!'

Akka sprang to my rescue. 'Who will ask questions? If anyone does, I'll take care of him.'

I don't blame Mama; I was of no help to him. On the contrary, he was the butt of many insults and jokes everyday on account of me. Who would tolerate such nonsense?

I came to a decision, tellling him I was leaving right then. It was eleven o'clock at night.

At just that moment the phone rang—Murugabhupati.

'Congratulations! I am speaking from Madurai. I have found a sponsor for your PhD, and I called you immediately.'

'Anna, I don't want to do any PhD now. I am going back to Pune. The situation here is not OK.'

Murugabhupati panicked and told me, 'Don't do anything in haste. Sleep over it. We'll discuss it tomorrow. Or you come over to Madurai now.'

'I don't want to study. Can you get me a job?'

'Wait till tomorrow and come to Madurai. We'll talk it over.'

I made a general announcement. 'I will go tomorrow. I don't want to be a burden to anyone here.'

Mama was very hurt.

'Can't you see that I said what I said for your good? Why don't you understand? Who will employ a person like you in a sari?

Even while Mama was ranting and raving, I found new mental strength. With greater conviction I said, 'I will get a job.'

'I'll find employment. I'll prove myself,' I told myself. 'At least for the sake of my anxious family and my supportive friends, I must get a job. I must—I will.'

That night I lay in sleepless hope.

A job for me

Next morning, I left my sister's house as planned, swept up in a whirlpool of emotions until I boarded the bus to Madurai. It seemed I could only blame either the world or myself for my situation, but I was unable to do either. I decided to let bygones be bygones and watch out for the future.

I reached the Mattudavani bus terminus, from where I called Murugabhupati. He asked me to meet him at the Periyar bus stand. Once I reached there, I found Gopi waiting for me. I was very happy to see him. A postgraduate student in the department of drama of Pondicherry University at the same time I was doing my MA, Gopi lived for theatre. In addition to having worked in many of Murugabhupati's productions, he had directed a few plays himself. He was expected to play an important role in the transition of Tamil theatre to the next stage.

Accompanying Gopi was another friend, Kannan, from Madurai, who had a master's degree in Tamil. I knew him through Murugabhupati's dramatic troupe. They took me to Murugabhupati's hotel room, carrying my heavy luggage.

Gathered in that tiny, untidy hotel room in one of the busy streets around the bus terminus were a number of Murugabhupati's theatre friends. To my surprise, I found Konangi—the Tamil author, and Murugabhupati's brother.

That Konangi Annan and Bhupati were happy to see me after a long gap was obvious from their expressions. The Saravanan they knew in the past was now a woman—Vidya. The brothers were incomparable in their maturity and understanding of other people. As soon as they made eye contact with you, they could instantly share your pain. They embraced me with great compassion.

'You are an artist, an angel. You should be our energy,' Bhupati said.

The dam burst and tears flowed down my cheeks at this demonstration of love and affection by my friends, which came as a balm to the emotional wounds I had accrued since my return from Pune.

My theatre friends were a group of happy people, who were together wherever they went. Lack of money was never a problem with them—they managed with what they had and what they could get, never complaining about their lives.

They were all men. I was the only woman in the room. The problem of where I would spend the night was solved by an invitation from Kannan, who lived with his family in Madurai.

I spent the night at Kannan's place along with Gopi and Malaichami. In the morning, they took me to Rajan Sir, the man who came forward to sponsor my PhD. He was working in Doordarshan, the government-run television network. When we arrived, he renewed his offer of sponsorship, but I politely declined, asking him instead for help in my efforts to find employment.

In the evening, we went to watch a Kashmiri dance drama—a brilliantly acrobatic performance—as part of a theatre festival at Raja Muthiah Hall.

The play was followed by pleasant conversation and dinner, after which we eventually wound our way to Kannan's house. My friends were optimistic about my employment prospects.

Kannan vacated his bedroom for me and slept in the hall with his friends, but I could not sleep at all that night. My life was so uncertain. My friends were much more helpful than my family—I did not want to burden them long with my problems. Confusion reigned supreme in my mind.

When I woke up and came out in the morning, I found Kannan sweeping the floor in front of the house. I realized I had overslept after a sleepless night.

After lunch, we had more conversations. I shared my experiences in Pune, the tirunangai lifestyle, culture, codes and signals with my friends.

The theatre festival went on for ten days. Bhupati went to his home town, Tirunelveli, after the festival; Gopi returned to Pondicherry; one by one, all the rest dispersed to different places, until only Kannan and I remained in Madurai. Malaichami, who stayed in the city with his friends, visited us often. Anxiety over my future was ever-present, but I triumphed over it thanks to my friends' love.

My sister Radha called a couple of times, and I reassured her.

'Don't worry, Akka. I'll soon get a job with the help of my friends.' My confidence was not entirely genuine.

When Kannan's siblings and mother—who had been away—came back, I had to find a new home. Murugabhupati then arranged for me to stay in a hotel room, but I was quite disturbed by this. How long would I flit from place to place with no feeling of security? Bhupati continued his job-hunting efforts through some NGOs he knew.

He put me on to Amudan, who ran a film society called 'Marupakkam', and had made documentary films on the lives and tribulations of Dalits. He offered to place me with an NGO serving tirunangais. I refused his offer because I was unhappy with the way most of these bodies functioned. My objection to their work was directed at their excessive focus on HIV/ AIDS awareness, while their main objectives should be the general welfare of transgenders, the redressal of their grievances, providing them job opportunities and economic freedom overall.

No Indian NGO had fought to liberate tirunangais from begging and sex work. What kind of rehabilitation was it to tell them, 'Go on being sex workers, but do it safely?'

I told Amudan I was totally against joining one of those NGOs. He then took me to an organization called People's Watch, which was involved in human rights issues. Amudan explained my problems to a female officer, who again tried to place me in an NGO for tirunangais. I declined her help and asked her at least find me a place to stay. She thought hard for a while and finally sent me on to a lady who gave refuge to destitute women.

I sent Murugabhupati off at the bus stand and went with Malaichami to Kannan's house to collect my personal effects. Malaichami and I set off to find the lady benefactor who would end my search for a place to stay. What a shock awaited me! The woman had vacated the place, and no one knew her whereabouts. We searched high and low, but all our efforts were in vain. Finally, beyond tears, I called Amudan and handed the phone to Malaichami when he wanted to speak to him. Malaichami spoke to Amudan and turned to me. 'Your problems are over. Let's make a last ditch effort.' He then made me board the Koripalayam bus with him.

Everyone called her Auntie. To me she was more like an angel. When I reached her house with Malaichami, she was waiting with an excellent meal she had cooked for us. She was Vijaya Auntie, who was to wipe away my tears and offer me refuge at a crucial stage of my life, protecting me like me a goddess.

At forty-five years of age, she effortlessly did what my family and friends could not. As active as a young girl, always smiling and easygoing by nature, she was an aunt not only to me but to countless others—especially the children of Krishnapuram Colony, where she lived. Though she did not know me at all, she readily welcomed me when my friends asked her to take me in. She made me a member of her family and I made her home my own.

Auntie made no enquiries about me, but welcomed me with open arms. Her own life had been no bed of roses. She had had to leave her husband and a turbulent marriage, with two children in tow. After many years as a successful single mother, she married again—a man she loved this time. Her life was an amazing story for her generation.

When I moved in with her, Auntie's eldest was already married. Her son was working in a courier service after finishing tenth standard in school. Her husband, who was working in another town, visited the family every weekend.

If Auntie's acceptance of me as a daughter was surprising, the way the rest of the family accepted me as well was nothing short of astonishing. I have never seen a happier, more united family. They gave me a place to stay like normal people. I had nice people for company, and peace and quiet to savour.

For the first time since my return from Pune, I was sleeping well. When I woke up in the morning, Auntie was invariably ready with a hot cup of coffee for me. Why did she and her family shower affection on me? What did I do to deserve their love and protection?

Not a day passed without my feeling grateful to Vijaya Auntie. She was always there in times of trouble, not only for me but the whole neighbourhood—a rare person, an avatar, a blessing.

There was now a bloom in my looks that friends began to notice. My only detriment was my continued unemployment. My friends were still busy searching for work on my behalf. One day, Amudan paid me a surprise visit.

'Wow! You have changed so much! I am so happy to see you look so well.' He had brought with him the addresses of many volunteer organizations, with directions for how to reach them, which buses to take, whom to meet, so on and so forth.

I knocked on the doors of almost every NGO in Madurai. The answer was always negative, though some of them were very tactful. But I never gave up. I went on applying for jobs, some even in private sector firms.

I met Ashok, a friend of Amudan's, at a bookstall. His concern really touched me. It was moving to know that so many people in a largely apathetic society spared time to help a tirunangai.

Ashok took me to an office in the Ellis Nagar area, behind the Periyar bus terminus. It was a small private bank that lent money to poor people. After a brief wait, we met the manager—he was a tall, dark man with curly hair, whose eyes shined bright with goodness.

His name was Anand Kumar, and he was a friend of Ashok's. I introduced myself, providing information about my experience. He asked me some questions about my education and what kind of work I could do at the bank.

'Do you think you can do field work? Or would you prefer desk work?' he asked me. Though I was interested in field work, I preferred to start with desk work, and I told him so. Anand Kumar then asked me to leave my resume and passport-size photograph with him. 'Let me discuss your case with the corporate office.'

When I went home, I told Auntie, 'This was the first meaningful interview I have attended. I am hopeful I'll get the job.'

'I'll be happy if you get it, but don't lose heart if you don't. Keep applying for jobs,' she advised me.

Four days later, I received a phone call from Anand Kumar.

'Can you attend an interview at our corporate office at Coimbatore?'

I said yes without a moment's hesitation.

Anand Kumar promised to call back after confirming with his office.

I went to Coimbatore the next day, happy and nervous at the same time. I kept all my friends informed—their good wishes adorned me as I entered the interview.

The managing director, Mr Udayakumar, interviewed me. He was a very simple man, and treated me not as a tirunangai, but as a fellow human. To his questions about my education, habits, typing speed and related matters, I answered truthfully.

'We have no problem with your being a transgender, but how will you handle teasing and harassment by people on your way to work?' he said. 'Will the office be subjected to problems?'

I began my reply with a smile. 'I don't anticipate any problem, sir. Even now, on my way here, some people at the autorickshaw stand teased me. I went straight to them and asked for an auto to bring me here. They were respectful after that and brought me here without incident. Much depends on the way we behave. Of course, there are incorrigible elements everywhere. We must take all that in our stride.'

'When are you joining?' he asked next.

I can never forget that moment. 'I'll join tomorrow, sir,' I told him happily. My job-hunting had been a penance. It was finally bearing fruit.

The MD congratulated me and had the company car drop me at the bus stand.

My happiness knew no bounds. It was as if I had been a captive for ages and had finally been released. I called all my friends and informed them. Their congratulations filled my ears.

I got into the bus, my mind and heart in flight. The bus could hardly keep pace.

A new journey

The bank was a micro-credit institution that lent to self-help groups promoted by NGOs. It had branches all over Tamil Nadu and Tiruvananthapuram. I was appointed an EDP assistant in the Madurai branch.

My branch manager, Anand Kumar, was an unusual man. Was he a man born to help people, or did he turn out that way through his work experience in an NGO involved in helping the poor? His concern for people was clearly reflected in his attitude towards me. Not once did he treat me differently because I am a tirunangai. He gave me the respect due to a colleague and encouraged me in my work.

My boss's helpful attitude made me happy and relaxed. Following his example, my other colleagues treated me as an equal. People like Tempavani, Ramar Pandi, Manjumati, Suresh Kumar, Muthuram, Palani, Kamalabhagyam and Muthamizhselvi were employees whose camaraderie meant a great deal to me. They never considered me a destitute, tirunangai or sinner. Their friendliness towards me was natural, not contrived. They were good people in a world of mercenaries.

Tempavani, slightly younger than me, is a woman I respect a great deal. Simple, competent, responsible, she was an active participant in all office activities. I used to accompany her on field work after lunch, and she was liked by all, including the villagers to whom she explained our schemes with great skill on these field trips. A steady worker, she was easily understood even by simple, illiterate folk.

Suresh Kumar was our senior field officer. Very capable, he had a keen interest in literature. He and I engaged in literary discussion at the office, and were—because of that—the butt of office jokes. 'There they go off!' was an oft heard remark. Ramar Pandi was another field officer—very keen to learn, and hard working. Two other field officers, Muthamizhselvi and Kamalabhagyam, came to Madurai on transfer from our Kanyakumari branch. Kamala, who attended college with Tempavani for agriculture, was also similarly sweet and simple. Muthamizh aspired to become an IPS officer like Kiran Bedi, and walked around smartly in pantsuits and close-cropped hair.

Palani, our office helper, was the jewel in the crown. We all depended so heavily on him that on days he was on leave, the office went to pieces. He was like a brother to me—a loving man. He knew computers like a college graduate, becoming proficient with them by watching me at work and asking questions.

I soon made friends in Madurai, mostly in the literary circles. Walking from office to Bharati Book Stall at the Periyar Bus Terminus, I used to meet Chezhian Uncle, Ravi, Arogyam, Stalin and others. All of them encouraged me to write. I wrote of my Pune experiences in a little magazine called *Mozhi*, brought out by my friends.

My life in Madurai was balm to my earlier struggles. Loving Vijaya Auntie, my caring office colleagues, and my literary friends gave me such comfort.

I was slowly emerging from the dark recesses of my life—I was happy. How true is the saying that all troubles come to pass.

Sivaraj was a friend I met through Nehru. He invited me

to attend an event he had arranged in Chennai, in which a physically handicapped musician was to be honoured. I lit the lamp at that gigantic event at the Kamarajar Hall.

It was at that program that I met Balabharati.

'Hi, I'm Bala,' he introduced himself. I extended my greetings. His transparent behaviour was very attractive, and we became friends. In time, we often discussed the problems of tirunangais.

One day, he suggested to me that I start writing about my experiences and the issues I was concerned about. I tried to fend him off by saying that finding publishers would be difficult, even though some of my writings had appeared in the little magazine, *Mozhi*. He then asked me a few questions: Was I educated? Did I read? Did I know the suffering of transgenders? Did I know computers? When I replied in the affirmative to all his questions, Balabharati suggested I start blogging.

Bala was not a highly educated man, but had a social conscience—he was a fighter. Someone who spent time and effort on issues of importance, he lent me his technical knowledge to set up my blog. Soon my blog was in place: http://livingsmile. blogspot.com.

My early posts on the blog were introductory pieces about me. Later, to my own surprise and pleasure, I wrote a couple of verses. I then joined a group called Tamizhmanam. My blog friends grew in number and variety quite rapidly: Divakar, Pons, Perasiriar, Dharumi, Ram, Mutturaman, Luckylook, Azhiyuran, Yogan Paris, and Sentazhal Ravi were some of my blogmates. They all encouraged me to continue writing.

Vijaya Auntie had to leave for the US to be with her brother, who was a doctor and had many friends in the Tamil literary field. I decided to leave her house because I was scared to stay there alone. I decided to move into a women's hostel, for my bank had connections with many NGOs. Anand sir, Suresh sir and Tempavani tried their best to find me accommodation in a girls' hostel, but to no avail. Most of them were hesitant to let me stay there for fear of offending the other inmates. Back to Square One!

Chezhian uncle asked me to try my luck with the Tamil Nadu Theological Seminary & TTS. The society had three men's hostels and one for women, which admitted girls from outside the institution as well.

The hostel was very reluctant to accommodate a transgender, but after much persuasion, decided to allow me to stay in a guest room, on a temporary trial basis. My first five days there were peaceful. I left for work early in the morning and spent my evenings quietly in the room, listening to music or reading. In the meantime, the college committee approved my request for permission to stay.

I had room no. 26 on the second floor. It had an attached bathroom with running water and a nice broad window, outside of which stood a tall neem tree. I had a view of the hostel garden, full of guava, lemon and neem trees—a lovely patch of green.

My expectations were simple: I wanted to live a normal life like all men and women. My being a tirunangai was natural, just as men are men, women are women, and cats are cats. Trouble arises when people do not understand this simple truth. We cannot even describe our problems as those of the minorities. All we need is equal opportunity to work and earn a livelihood. Only when people approach us with evil intent and harass us do we have to take specific steps with negative outcomes.

Please believe me when I say that most of the violent behaviour of tirunangais in public places—their loud talk and aggressive soliciting, for instance—is out of self-defence.

We live in a world which offers us no security. Only by

doing something disgusting can we keep at bay men who are much stronger than we are. We can't even go to the police when we are assaulted, sexually or otherwise. They don't take our complaints seriously.

Most tirunangais are unlettered. Thus, they cannot find avenues of expression as I have done. Even if they are prepared for hard work, they have few skills. Who will help them if they want to study?

We need to belong, just as the rest of humanity needs to belong. What can we do when we don't have a wall to lean on, when we can't find a place to stay?

I poured out all I knew in my blog, based on my own experience. My writing had an impact on many people, with far-reaching effects.

The editor of *Aval Vikatan*, who had heard about my employment and stay in a hostel, contacted me with a view to featuring me in the magazine.

I was not overly enthused by magazine articles on me, but I was happy that a women's magazine was interested in me as a woman. It was an acknowledgment of my womanhood.

Before the article, I had only two friends in the hostel—Malar and her roommate. Now many readers, affected by the story, were viewing me like a celebrity. My friends' circle kept growing larger all the while. I had to explain to all of them that the only thing I sought was friendship. One friend I enjoyed meeting was eighteen-year-old Nandini from Sri Lanka. Whenever she sought me out to chat with me, time flew.

As my hostel did not have a proper mess, I decided to learn to cook, something I did not have to attempt while staying with Vijaya Auntie. I had had, though, a few cooking lessons with Auntie before she left for the US. Around this time, a number of magazines started publishing feature stories about me.

It was the end of a nightmare: I had friends everywhere. What more did I want?

Balabharati arranged for me to visit his friends, Joseph and Malati, a couple who feared tirunangais like most ordinary people do. Thanks to Bharati, I spent a whole day with them, dispelling their fears, and making friends with them and their ten-year-old daughter. It was a revelation to them, and they accepted me as a friend.

I attended many literary meetings in Madurai and surrounding towns. I met Ilangovan and Geeta while delivering a lecture at Nallor Vattam, and they became good friends who introduced me to many more, going so far as to enroll me in a women's group engaged in reading sessions. Gradually, I was to shed all my inhibitions and emerge into an active and useful social life.

Office work, field work, conversations with my friends during leisure hours, friendship with my hostel mates and finally my active internet life—all made me happy and fulfilled; yet there was an inner voice all the while that I could not seem to still.

Social acceptance of tirunangais did not end with my rehabilitation.

I want to live—with pride

I came back from Pune not merely to find employment, but to confirm my identity—my Self.

I mention freedom and independence throughout this book, and what I mean when I use these words includes legally enforceable social status.

As a first step, I wanted to change my name from Saravanan to Living Smile Vidya. I applied to the Tamil Nadu Stationery and Printing Department. When asked to give my reason for changing my name, I mentioned my sex change operation. My application was returned after a few days carrying the remark, 'Applications without a reason assigned cannot be entertained.'

I went to a lawyer to help me change my name officially. She was Madurai's best advocate and a feminist thinker, who had—along with tirunangai Priya Babu—filed a public interest litigation demanding franchise for tirunangais. The judgment was indecisive: tirunangais could choose male or female as their gender, an important victory for transgenders. Some of them had voter ID cards as a result.

But the right to vote alone does not empower tirunangais. It cannot improve their day-to-day life. Unless they can change their names and sex in their school and other certificates, they are not employable. They can't even open bank accounts. So, I asked advocate Rajini to get my name changed.

Following her advice, I sent petitions to my district collector, taluk office and the chief secretariat, seeking help to have my name and sex changed in all my papers.

A few days later, I received a letter from the Srirangam taluk office asking me to present myself there. Though it was my birthplace, I had to search hard before I located the building. After some waiting I was brought in to meet the officers.

I explained my problem all over again.

'Where's your ration card?

'I don't have a ration card, and my family won't give it to me.'

'Please leave your address here. We'll have to investigate.' My request was forwarded to the Tamil Nadu Stationery and Printing Department, and that gave me hope. My hope was short-lived, however, as the department demanded a medical certificate from me.

I wrote a detailed letter again explaining how my sex change operation had no legal sanction, and how an independent medical certificate had mentioned the event. Pat came the reply: 'We cannot recognize an operation that was performed without government approval. We cannot accede to your request for change of name.'

I went to court, as I had no other option. The court decreed that my request for change of name be examined. So I waited once again in hope.

There were reports then of a proposal to allow sex change operations in government hospitals. The tirunangais could pursue studies after that, armed with the necessary name change certificates. I waited.

Despite the court order, the Stationery and Printing Department refused to examine my request for change of name. After continued arguments, they finally asked me to produce a medical certificate from Madurai Medical College.

It took some time for their letter to reach the Madurai Rajaji Medical College. I hung around there for ten days, unfazed by all the harassment and ridicule, and literally forced them to test me medically. At last I collected the certificate.

It took me a year and a half to change my name—to exercise my legal, moral right. How hard I had to fight—how many rounds to various hospitals, advocates, taluk office, collectorate and Stationery and Printing Department I had to undertake to accomplish my purpose—when politicians, people who believe in numerology, people who convert from religion to religion, can change their names in a month!

Everywhere I went, I had to suffer barbs, ignore insults, brush aside hurts. On my way home from work, there was always the jibe or two flung at me—'Hey, is this a boy or a girl?' While all around laughed at me, I tried to hide my tears.

Not just men, but sometimes women, too, laughed at me. Every time that happened, I swallowed my pride, hid my irritation and walked on. At supermarkets, fruit shops, bakeries, villains sprang up from nowhere to torment me.

Even kids didn't spare me. Once they followed me when I was on field duty and sang raucous film songs at me. Who taught them to do this? Where did they learn such domineering behaviour? If you see a tirunangai, attack her, insult her, make her cry; chase her away whimpering, screaming—that seemed to be the rule, regardless of race, religion or creed.

What had I done to any of these people? I never applied so much make-up that I attracted attention. What they saw was my natural body.

My sex, my skin colour—all were natural. Why did people never understand?

I hated this lot. My irritation and annoyance threatened

to become a permanent part of my life. All my journeys in Madurai ended in disaster. They made me feel I was in hell. Men and women either eyed me lasciviously or laughed at me in an uncivilized manner—even children spewed poison at me.

Madurai is an overgrown village—I could not escape such uncultured behaviour there. I thought it would be wiser to move to a metropolis like Chennai. My own personal security, which my Madurai job gave me, ceased to be satisfying. I quit to go to Chennai, where I could fight for a better deal for tirunangais.

In Chennai, I stayed at Arunammal's house and started looking for a job with Senthil's help. They both gave me shelter and support when I was broke—I can never forget that. Soon I found a dream job; after I relaxed my self-imposed ban on working for an NGO, I was given the opportunity of working in the administrative wing of Suyam Trust.

Suyam is a family, a magic world, that embraces all who come for refuge with love. Mutturaman and Uma are parents to all the destitute children who seek their help. The couple has been helping such orphaned children since their college days. Located in Pazhavedupettai, their Siragu Montessori School was started with the dream of providing free quality education—some three hundred children have benefited from its existence. What a wonderful achievement!

In a happy place, secure in a friendly atmosphere, with great job satisfaction and a normal life, only my efforts to gain my identity are still unsuccessful. I am not Saravanan—I am Vidya. Is the government listening?

India freed herself sixty-six years ago. Amidst our achievements and failures, democracy has remained strong and intact. Dalits have a voice, feminists are heard—they can hold rallies, demand their rights. But transgenders are the Dalits of Dalits, the most oppressed women among women—they enjoy no equality, no freedom, no fraternity. They continue to lead a wretched life, devoid of pride and dignity.

Very rarely do people even talk about us or write about us. Are we so undeserving? I cannot understand.

We grow up in families amidst parents, siblings and relatives. The day we realize our difference and try to express it, we are driven out mercilessly. Does anyone have the minimum awareness about us? We are objects of ridicule; film songs treat us as freaks. Every time I come across such lewdness, my blood boils. Why can't people who depict us so understand our pain and suffering? Society marginalizes us constantly. Tirunangais have no family, no jobs, no security, nothing.

These nowhere people gather together in India's different states and form a family, or families, with their own rules, their own traditions and rituals—they laugh and cry together; they somehow manage to eke out a communal living.

Hunger: but for that, no tirunangai would beg on the streets, trains, at marketplaces. They submerge pride and dignity and put their hands out in supplication, seeking alms, only because all windows of opportunity are closed to them. It is our tragedy that the world does not understand this simple truth.

It is not improbable that a male-dominated society cannot tolerate a man wanting to become a woman. Women who have accepted male domination tend to agree with that view. The presence of a tirunangai in a family is considered a disgrace: they are believed to hamper a family's progress and restrict their normal activities.

All I want is legal approval and recognition that will enable us to walk freely in public. Why can't governments think on these lines? Why can't we legalize the sex change operation, when tirunangais cannot help being what they are—when they cannot change nature? Why can't we fall in line with other nations, where such operations are legal?

There is a government order (Order No. 377) that treats transgenders as disease-afflicted sex workers alone. This must be removed, and sex reassignment surgery must be allowed for those medically and psychologically tested and certified transgender. Reservation could be considered, too. This is what we seek from the government as minimum aid.

At schools, in the Arivoli Iyakkam, in other non-formal schools, tirunangais can be introduced to students as part of their lessons, so that they learn to treat difference with compassion and dignity. Children should be told about the suffering of transgenders. Film censor boards must firmly root out scenes depicting them in a vulgar manner.

The government can do it. If it will—if the government takes one step—society will follow suit. Once we gain social approval, our families will also accept us. Politicians take out flag marches for a million causes. They can surely take some interest in this issue?

I do not ask for heaven—I am begging to be spared from living hell. I plead for myself and fellow tirunangais. Thank you for your understanding.

33407634R00086

Printed in Great Britain
by Amazon